I0802416

Integrating **Growth Mindset** *in* ***Schools***

Strategies and Scripts for Bringing Growth Mindset to Your Learning Community

NATIONAL CENTER for YOUTH ISSUES

P.O. Box 22185
Chattanooga, TN 37422-2185
423-899-5714 • 866-318-6294
fax: 423-899-4547
www.ncyi.org

ISBN: 978-1-937870-48-5 $27.95
Library of Congress Control Number: 2018936723

Written by: Lisa King, Ed.S, LPC
Contributing Editor: Jennifer Deshler
Design: Phillip Rodgers
Published by National Center for Youth Issues

Printed at Starkey Printing, Chattanooga, Tennessee, U.S.A., April 2018

TABLE OF CONTENTS

Chapter 1: **Introduction to Integrating Growth Mindset in Schools**

This chapter provides an easy-to-read overview of what growth mindset is, and why it is needed in schools. Additionally, there is a literature review of the research conducted over the past 10 years showing how growth mindset has a positive impact on student achievement.

Chapter 2: **Professional Development on Growth Mindset**

This chapter explains how schools can adopt a growth mindset initiative, along with examples for school leaders to use in setting up both development and breakout sessions for school staff.

Section 1: Grades K-8

Section 2: Grades 9-12

Chapter 3: **Easy-to-Implement Parent Workshops on Growth Mindset**

This chapter offers several ways to structure parent workshops, along with accompanying PPTs and scripts so that school leaders can use to run Parent Workshops.

Section 1: Parent Workshop Ideas Grades K-8

Section 2: Parent Workshop Ideas Grades 9-12

Chapter 4: **Growth Mindset Infused in School-Wide Programs**

This chapter offers several ways to structure parent workshops, along with accompanying PPTs and scripts so that school leaders can use to run Parent Workshops.

CHAPTER ONE

1

Introduction to Integrating Growth Mindset in Schools

Introduction

Integrating Growth Mindset in Schools and *Mindset Matters*: Companion Books to Roll Out a Growth Mindset Initiative in your School

After releasing *Mindset Matters* and hearing from school counselors, it became clear that many were looking for help beginning a growth mindset program in their schools. Both books are meant to spark ideas of how teaching growth mindset can work in your school, but think of *Mindset Matters* as a companion curriculum to this book.

What you will find in this book:

Integrating Growth Mindset into Schools

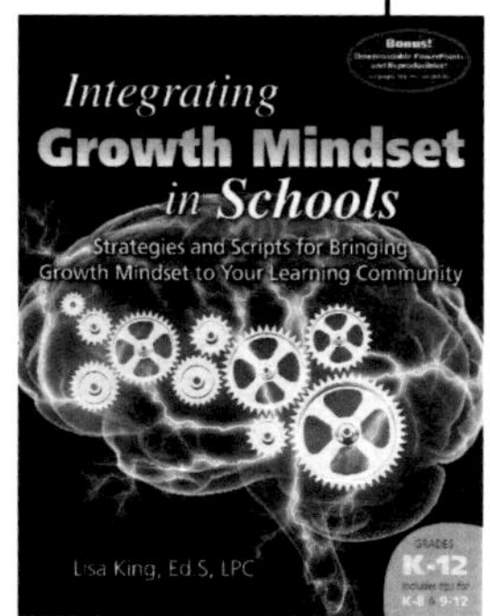

In this resource (geared for Grades K-12) educators have PPTs that can be downloaded and used with a script to present Parents Workshops, Staff Development, and concise one-time growth mindset lessons to students, and small group ideas.

This book includes:

- Parent Workshop Outline on Growth Mindset (with PPT/script)
- Staff Professional Development Outline on Growth Mindset (with PPT/script)
- Single Lesson Outline for Implementing a Classroom Lesson on Growth Mindset (with PPT/script)
- Mini-Posters
- Innovative and Interactive Lessons for group and classroom

Like what you see? Check out the companion book!

Mindset Matters

If your school already has begun a growth mindset program and you are working with Grades 2-7 and want a good structure for teaching growth mindset, then *Mindset Matters* is the book for you. This resource focuses on providing an outline for you to teach growth mindset with a choice of over 60 lessons to choose from. By using the letters in the word MINDSET, an acrostic guides lessons taught as shown in the topics below. For any educator teaching Social Emotional Learning (SEL), this book will provide ideas to structure a year, a semester, or a unit in an impactful way .

Mindset Matters includes:

- Bibliotherapy Ideas Video Index
- Lessons for SEL /Classroom Core Curriculum and Small Groups on Growth Mindset by breaking it down into the following topics:
  - Mindfulness
  - Identifying Brain Basics
  - Not Yet Is OK
  - Determination and Grit
  - Self-Talk
  - Everyone is Unique
  - Teach Others What You Know

The Basics: Growth Mindset 101

A vast amount of research has been done to show the many benefits of teaching growth mindset theory to students. Dr. Carol Dweck, the pioneer of growth mindset and a professor at Stanford University, tells us that people with a growth mindset are more likely to have motivation and succeed. Growth mindset has become a popular idea that is not only interesting for kids to learn about but is also beneficial for staff and parents to understand and implement in their own spheres of influence. Within this curriculum, you will find ideas of how to integrate growth mindset into your school in a way that best serves your students and your community.

What is Growth Mindset?

Mindset is a concept brought to light by Dr. Carol Dweck. In her research, she determined that there are two types of mindset, or the way we approach things.

1. Growth Mindset is the belief that people can get smarter and increase their intelligence with deliberate practice. Growth mindset is the understanding that the brain can continuously grow.
2. Fixed Mindset is the belief that people are born with a certain amount of talent and intelligence and that there is a limit to success based on innate ability.

If Someone Has a Growth Mindset, What Skills are Likely to Improve?

- sticking with difficult tasks
- accepting and welcoming challenges
- seeing mistakes as learning opportunities
- seeking and listening to feedback
- practicing and using strategies to improve
- having the curiosity to dive into learning
- taking risks to try new things

Purpose of This Book

When people learn about growth mindset, they get excited about it. You can find a vast amount of information and ideas on growth mindset anywhere from a Google search, to YouTube videos, podcasts, and ongoing scholarly research. Sometimes there is an "information overload" which needs to be narrowed down to understand so much material. In the curriculum called *Mindset Matters* (2016), I used the letters from the word MINDSET to create an acrostic with the principle concepts of growth mindset (see figure A).

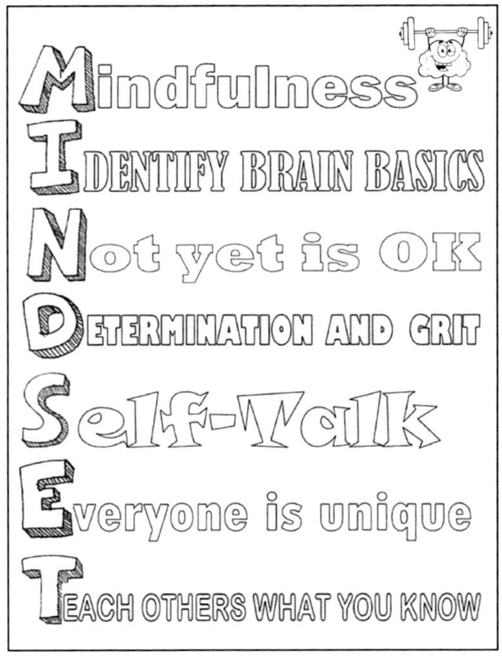

Figure A (Poster found on page 102)

It has become clear these concepts of growth mindset resonate with teachers, administrators, auxiliary staff, parents and students. It is a theory people are drawn to know more about because it naturally connects to so many of the programs we are already doing in our schools and can apply to our own lives. The purpose of this book is to provide a user-friendly way for schools to weave growth mindset ideas into programs we are already doing: state-wide testing, college and career readiness, parent workshops, collecting data and more. I also wanted to continue the concepts of *Mindset Matters* and expand them to be applicable to K-12 for lessons, programs, parent workshops, professional development as well as student lessons and programs.

If you are not familiar with the basics of growth mindset, it is worthwhile to listen to Carol Dweck's TED Talk called "The Power of Believing that You Can Improve." She says teaching growth mindset and the power of yet can empower kids. "We're finding just the words 'yet' or 'not yet' give kids greater confidence and give them a path into the future that creates greater persistence. And we can actually change students' mindsets."

The continued interest of the educational community in learning about growth mindset is the result of ongoing research that tells us how it benefits students. Becoming a school that undertakes growth mindset as an initiative is easier when there is a curriculum to help you streamline the process. This curriculum offers teachers, counselors and administrators with a user-friendly program to teach students that **intelligence can grow, and with hard work, there are endless possibilities to what can be accomplished.**

How to Use This Book

This book will help make integrating growth mindset into your school easy with high impact results. Realistically, some schools might start with a baby step of introducing the concepts to students and then publicizing the positive results to get more buy-in. Perhaps the next year a parent workshop can be introduced. You will find that growth mindset theory is easy to infuse into your school because it's likely you can integrate the concepts into things you are doing already, such as testing skills or college readiness. The planning tool on page 15 will help you customize the program roll-out that is right for you.

Consider integrating growth mindset into your school like going to a buffet…take what you like. Come back later and try something new next time.

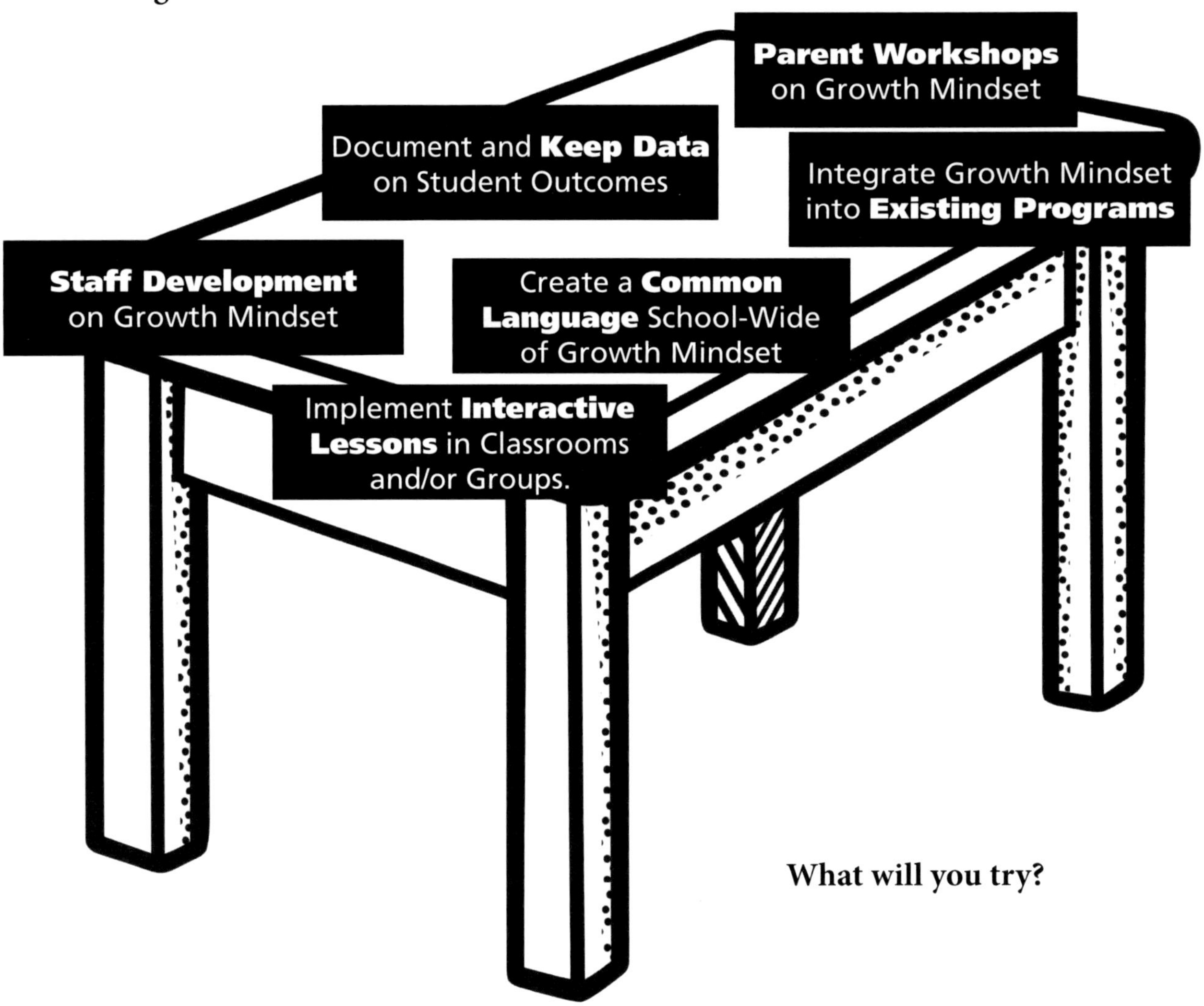

What will you try?

What Are the Features that Make this Book User-friendly?

This icon indicates an email you can download, personalize, and send out for your program.

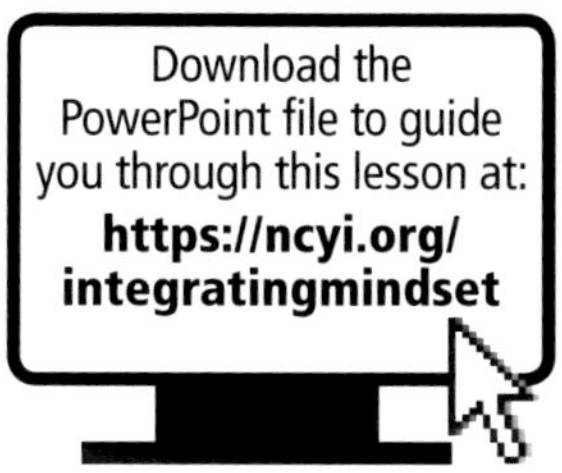

This icon indicates a PowerPoint you can download and use for lessons, professional development sessions, and/or parent workshops.

This icon indicates a video on this subject that can be used as a supplement in your lesson.

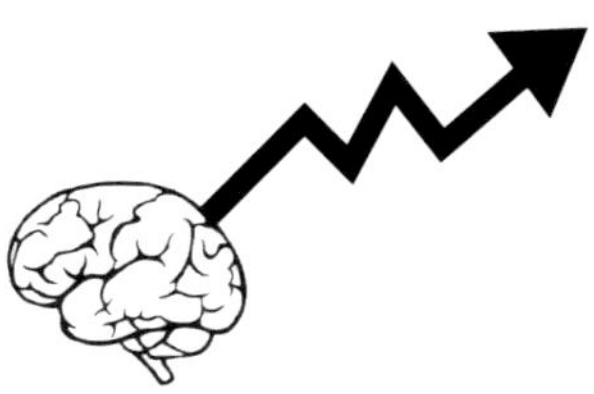

This icon indicates data you can collect and report, showing that your intervention, program, or lessons are leading to results.

Ideas for Rolling Out the Curriculum

If your school wants to implement a Growth Mindset Curriculum, here is a model of how to roll out the program over two school years. See page 15 to use the planning tool to personalize the roll out with your school team. Below are some recommendations for a roll out, but each school should customize to their needs.

K-8 Roll Out of Growth Mindset Curriculum Sample

(x= recommended ? = optional)

	YEAR ONE	YEAR TWO
Establish/Maintain School Wide Common Language of Growth Mindset	X	X
Staff Professional Development on Growth Mindset	X	X
Reinforce Growth Mindset In Existing Programs		X
Collect Data to Document Student Growth	X	X
Implement Counselor or Teacher Driven Lessons on Growth Mindset • With a Pilot Group? • All Classrooms? • Target Group of Students?	X Pilot Classes* X Group	Classes Groups
Parent Workshop(s) on Growth Mindset		X
Focused Professional Development with New Teachers and Mentors		
Mindset Peer Mentors		?

9-12 Roll Out of Growth Mindset Curriculum Sample

(x= recommended ? = optional)

	YEAR ONE	YEAR TWO
Establish/Maintain School Wide Common Language of Growth Mindset	X	X
Staff Professional Development on Growth Mindset	X	X
Reinforce Growth Mindset In Existing Programs		X
Collect Data to Document Student Growth	X	X
Implement Counselor or Teacher Driven Lessons on Growth Mindset • With a Pilot Group? • All Classrooms? • Target Group of Students?	X Groups	Pilot Classes* Groups
Parent Workshop(s) on Growth Mindset		?
Focused Professional Development with New Teachers and Mentors		
Mindset Peer Mentors		X

*Pilot classes refer to a group of teachers or grade levels that might want to "champion" the program and implement a growth mindset curriculum as innovators and leaders.

PLANNING TOOL
Options for Rolling Out *Mindset Matters* School Wide

Use this planning tool for your team to decide what will work best for your school.

1. On the left, each team member should check off what is feasible to implement at your school. Each school is different so decide what will and won't work for you.
2. Next, move to the columns on the right and think about which 2-4 of these ideas to implement in Year One and Year Two.
3. After each team member fills out this planning tool, collaborate to discuss a final plan for rolling out the integration of growth mindset at your school.

Feasible?		YEAR ONE	YEAR TWO
	Establish/Maintain School Wide Common Language of Growth Mindset (i.e.: grit, neuroplasticity, the power of yet)		
	Staff Professional Development on Growth Mindset		
	Reinforce Growth Mindset In Existing Programs		
	Collect Data to Document Student Growth		
	Teach Student Lessons on Growth Mindset • With a Pilot Group? • All Classrooms? • Target Group of Students?		
	Parent Workshop(s) on Growth Mindset		
	Focused Professional Development with New Teachers and Mentors		
	Mindset Peer Mentors		

Growth Mindset Research Review
(Grades K-8)

FACT: Students who adopt a growth mindset significantly outperform peers who have a fixed mindset.

OVERRIDING QUESTION: Why WOULDN'T we teach growth mindset SKILLS to students?

RESEARCH DETAILS: A study conducted by Blackwell, Trzesniewski, and Dweck (2007) in New York City over a two-year period showed that students with a growth mindset showed more effort and were more resilient to obstacles. Students with a fixed mindset avoided challenges, gave up more easily, and did not accept feedback well. Also, over time the achievement gap widened and the students who had a growth mindset significantly outperformed their peers who had a fixed mindset.

FACT: Teacher mindset can influence student's test scores and attitude towards learning.

OVERRIDING QUESTION: Why WOULDN'T we teach about growth mindset to teachers?

RESEARCH DETAILS: Rheinberg (2000), measured the effect of teacher mindset on student achievement. He found that when teachers had a growth mindset, their low achieving students improved their grades and became moderate or even high achievers. He found that low achieving students with teachers with a fixed mindset on average remained low achievers.

FACT: Parents who praise their kids' effort in the learning process rather than a child's intelligence, help their children adopt a growth mindset.

OVERRIDING QUESTION: Why WOULDN'T we teach about growth mindset to parents?

RESEARCH DETAILS: A study by Schleider, Schroder, Lo et al (2016), indicates that parents with a fixed mindset instead of a growth mindset had children with greater anxiety who internalized problems more often. Additionally, the work of Mueller and Dweck (1998) demonstrated that adults who praise students' effort ("You are really trying hard.") versus intelligence ("You are so smart.") had children with higher achievement and motivation.

Sources:
- http://www.temescalassoc.com/db/el/files/2015/02/Growth-Mindsets-Lit-Review.pdf
- http://psycnet.apa.org/journals/psp/75/1/33/
- https://alumni.stanford.edu/get/page/magazine/article/?article_id=32124
- https://link.springer.com/article/10.1007/s10826-016-0513-7

Growth Mindset Research Review
(Grades 9-12)

FACT: Students who adopt a growth mindset have a higher likelihood of graduation.

OVERRIDING QUESTION: What data supports the concept that implementing growth mindset lessons impacts student outcome?

RESEARCH DETAILS: Studies found that when students had a growth mindset they had:

- Increased credits earned and on-time graduation.

Yeager et al. (2013) found that students who learned about growth mindset during their senior year of high school and the summer after, had an increased likelihood of earning 12+ credits during their first college term by 3-4% indicating a strong prediction of on-time graduation.

- Reduction in courses failed.

Over 1500 students in 13 high schools across the country who learned about growth mindset showed a reduced percentage of courses failed by low-achieving students by 7 percentage points, compared to control group of students. (Paunesku et al 2015). https://web.stanford.edu/~paunesku/articles/paunesku_2015.pdf

Growth Mindset Interventions and Results

From Gates Foundation "Academic Tenacity: Mindsets and Skills that Promote Long Term Learning (pg. 15)

AUTHORS	RESEARCH PARTICIPANTS	EFFECTS (RELATIVE TO CONTROL GROUP)
Teaching Students that Intelligence Can Be Developed (A Growth Mindset)		
Blackwell, Trzesniewski, & Dweck (2007)	Urban, Low-income, African American and Latino 7th grade students	Higher Math Grades
Good, Aronson, & Inzlicht (2003)	African American and Latino middle school students at a rural school	Higher state test scores for all grading and for girls in math
Aronson, Fried, & Good (2002)	African American and white college students	Higher GPA; greater valuing and enjoyment of academics

Cited from https://ed.stanford.edu/sites/default/files/manual/dweck-walton-cohen-2014.pdf

Getting Your School to Buy-In

When asked, "On a scale of 1-10, how open would your staff be to a growth mindset curriculum?", attendees at a conference were given a few minutes to discuss their answers.

As I asked for group feedback, a principal in the audience answered, "You have to make it seem like your teachers' idea." I couldn't help but laugh. Only moments before, I'd heard from another table, "You have to make it seem like it's your administrator's idea."

Isn't this true for any new initiative? Whoever's idea it is, you want the other party to "drink the Kool-Aid" and be so excited about the idea that they take ownership. But, how do you begin? The main step is to do something to plant the seed. You might need to start talking about it now and implement it next year or next semester. Take the first step in showing that you have a growth mindset about bringing innovation and "best practices" to your building. As you begin talking to colleagues about growth mindset with passion, many around you will get excited. In the next few pages are guidelines for you whether you are an administrator or teacher/counselor in how to proceed with getting staff buy-in.

Example of Growing a Program

In 2016-17, school counselor Becky Grindstaff introduced growth mindset into her school in grades 2-5 during counseling curriculum lessons using *Mindset Matters*. The staff saw increased Lexile level in reading (as per county reading inventory) as well as an increase in student perception of being able to deal with mistakes (as per a pre-post survey). The staff and administration decided in 2017-2018 to infuse the curriculum across Pre K-5th grade.

The feeder high school heard about what the elementary school was doing and wanted in on the positive outcomes. Becky met with the school council of Pope High School, which consists of parents, teachers, and administrators. Together, they came up with a plan to have a growth mindset initiative for the 2018-19 year in the high school, and planned to include the feeder middle school, as well.

How cool that the kids in that K-12 community had an opportunity to learn about all of the possibilities that can come with hard work, practice, and dealing with adversity; the growth mindset way?

Are You an **Administrator** Who Is Excited about Bringing Growth Mindset to Your School?

Here are some steps to take:

1. **Plan Dates**

   Planning is key. Getting dates on the calendar is essential, so that implementation and follow-up take place. Meet with your teacher leaders, and fellow administrators to get their input using the planning tool on page 15.

2. **Introduce the Topic to Staff in a User-Friendly Way**

   Show a video such as Carol Dweck's TED Talk. Your staff will enjoy learning in this format and will see an immediate connection to how this can benefit their students and others.

3. **Follow-Up with Staff**

   Reinforce the concepts of growth mindset throughout the year with emails and staff meetings. Intermittently remind staff of your expectation to see growth mindset concepts being taught in their classrooms.

4. **Follow Through with Students**

   Set up ways to reinforce important ideas of growth mindset with students, i.e. acknowledging students on morning announcements or in hallway displays.

5. **Connect Growth Mindset Concepts with Existing School Programs**

   When programs like College/Career Day, Anti-Bullying campaigns, or statewide testing come up in your school year, make sure to use these occasions to tie in growth mindset. Grit, learning from mistakes, and growing from adversity are great messages of growth mindset that can easily be connected to existing school programs.

6. **Celebrate Success**

   Acknowledge staff members who are going above and beyond with best practices to reinforce growth mindset in their classroom. Have staff members brainstorm what has been successful for them. Share any data that has been collected to show the benefits of implementing the teaching of growth mindset at your school.

Are You an **Educator** Who Is Excited about Bringing Growth Mindset to Your School?

Here are some steps to take:

1. **Get Administrator Buy-In**

   Take the first step by beginning a conversation about growth mindset with your administrator(s). If you watch any of the videos on the ideas of growth mindset, you will get excited. Bring that excitement with you to a meeting with your principal. Talk about data and the benefits for staff morale, and let your administrators know you are willing to help with either leading a book study, doing a training with your staff, or setting up a parent workshop. Start as small as you want, but begin talking about it and sharing the research. Invite your administrators to build a plan, using the planning tool (page 15).

2. **Set Some Dates on the Master Calendar**

   Once you have a foot in the door with your administrator, begin putting dates on the calendar. Formally plan specific dates for things like Growth Mindset Parent Night and/or Growth Mindset Staff Development. If you don't plan it, life will get busy and it won't get done.

3. **Plan Your Lessons and/or Groups**

   Plan class lessons and/or small groups. *Mindset Matters* (2016) is filled with many lesson ideas and there are other resources from which to draw inspiration. There are also lessons in this book, *Integrating Growth Mindset in Schools*. Create a framework for grade levels or groups you can do at your school.

4. **Connect Growth Mindset with Other Existing School-Wide Programs.**

   Let your administrator know how seamlessly concepts of growth mindset can link to already existing programs at your school. Grit, learning from mistakes, and dealing with adversity are great messages of growth mindset that can easily be connected to existing school programs such as: College/Career Day, Anti-Bullying campaigns, or statewide testing.

5. **Get Excited!**

   Enthusiasm is contagious, especially when coupled with research that shows the positive benefits of teaching growth mindset. Get excited about the positive effects you can have on attitudes and student achievement.

Email Samples to Promote a Growth Mindset Culture

Brief Sample Email to Administrator Introducing Growth Mindset

To: Administrator

Subject: New Idea- Growth Mindset

I wanted to touch base about some new ideas I've heard about that I think could benefit our school. The information I've been reading is very exciting about how we can integrate the theory of growth mindset into what we are already doing at ___________ school. Growth mindset is research-based, has been proven to increase achievement, and is easy to implement… win-win, right? You can preview Carol Dweck talking about growth mindset in this 10-minute TED Talk at http://bit.ly/2sbfCYc or check out the resources at http://bit.ly/2slHYPb.

When would be a good time when I can sit down and share some of the info with you? I'm excited about the impact growth mindset could have at our school!

Sincerely,

Detailed Sample Email to Administrator Introducing Growth Mindset

To: Administrator

Subject: Bringing Growth Mindset Here

Good Afternoon! I wanted to email you about a new professional learning initiative I would love to help bring to our school. I have heard strong results from other schools that have integrated growth mindset into their programs, and think it would be great here... and we could implement on a small scale or go big. I'm happy to take leadership, but first wanted to explain my thoughts to you and get your feedback.

If you haven't seen the TED Talk where Carol Dweck discusses growth mindset, you can watch at http://bit.ly/2sbfCYc or check out the resources at http:// bit.ly/2slHYPb.

My thoughts on what this can entail are as follows:

- Common Language: Creating a common way to talk about grit, the power of yet, and how hard deliberate practice leads to changes in intelligence.
- Staff Development: Research says that students benefit academically when their teachers adopt a growth mindset. Brief professional development could highlight the key points.
- Groups: Counselor-led or teacher-led small groups or mini-lessons can teach target groups of students the key concepts of growth mindset. Positive outcomes have been documented.
- Connection to other programs: Growth mindset connects to perseverance, STEM, college/career readiness, and preparing for high stakes testing. This is a great way to encourage students within a framework that is research-based.

As you can tell, I'm excited and would love to sit down and brainstorm how this can align with our school mission and benefit our community. Do you think we could find a time to sit down and talk more about this?

Look forward to talking soon.

Email to Staff Announcing Upcoming Professional Development

Subject: New Relevant Professional Development

Hello Team!

Our administrators want to support our professional learning time in the best way possible. They have invited us to get together and explore some research that is pertinent to all educators, regardless of what subject you teach. The theory that we will be exploring is called growth mindset- the concept that intelligence can change over time with hard work. We will be learning about some research-based ideas. These ideas include information about how grit, perseverance, and the ability to understand how the brain grows can affect achievement scores. How cool is that?! These meetings will be brief, practical, and relevant. At our first meeting, we will watch this 10 minute TED Talk video (feel free to preview...http://bit.ly/1wBJmZ6).

Look forward to learning with you all,

NOTE: The above email might be useful if your school has auxiliary school staff members in "singleton" roles (i.e.: ESOL teachers, speech therapists, art/music/PE). Sometimes, professional development opportunities are focused on math or writing curriculum that doesn't apply to these professionals and a growth mindset professional learning community might be perfect for this circumstance.

Not long ago, while presenting a workshop on *Mindset Matters* in my district, I had several colleagues who were interested in finding out more about integrating growth mindset into their schools. I invited these school counselors to get together and discuss how we might be able to collect data showing the impact of teaching growth mindset.

We accomplished this task, and came up with a comprehensive results report. During this same time, I had the pleasure of witnessing a rock star counselor, Becky Grindstaff, bring growth mindset to her school in what turned into a full implementation of a growth mindset initiative.

Think back to page 12, where I used the metaphor that starting a growth mindset program is like going to a buffet; on your first time through, take what you want to try and come back to try more later. At Tritt Elementary in Marietta, GA, Mrs. Grindstaff went to the buffet the first year and tried interactive lessons and on year two, they made it a priority, and tried it all. This unusual feat is awesome but will not be realistic for everyone.

Here is the outline of her school's initiative:

TRITT ELEMENTARY

Rebecca Grindstaff
Counselor,
School-wide Initiatives

Growth Mindsets School-Wide Monthly Themes:

- Mindfulness/ September
- Identify Brain Basics/ October
- Not Yet is OK/ November
- Determination/Grit/ December and January
- Self-Talk/ February
- Everyone is Unique/ March
- Teach Others What You Know/ April

Delivery Model:

Students: classroom lessons/ classroom meetings/ news programming/ bathrooms

Staff: read *Mindset Matters*, post planning in-service, tips in Friday Newsletter

Parents: parent night(s) planned, teachers will introduce initiative at Open House

As a staff we will praise students for:

Effort - embracing challenges with hard work

Strategy - highlight steps the student took in problem solving

Persistence - praise for pushing through frustration

CHAPTER TWO

2

Professional Development on Growth Mindset

Why Should Educators Have Professional Development on Growth Mindset?

We all remember that teacher who encouraged us to *want* to learn. We remember the feeling of wanting to impress that teacher. What made them so important to us? Many studies have been done about the traits teachers, who are most effective and inspirational, possess. This chapter will explore one of these traits: **teacher mindset**. Rheinberg (2000) did a study that showed teachers who have a growth mindset (the belief that intelligence is malleable and can grow with effort) had students who outperformed students in a classroom where the teacher held a fixed mindset (the belief that you are born with certain intelligences that won't change over time).

TOP FOUR REASONS TO TEACH EDUCATORS ABOUT GROWTH MINDSET:

1. Student Outcomes Improve

When teachers learn about the growth mindset research that enhances students' improvement, they learn the value of praising student effort. The language of praising effort vs. praising intelligence has shown to result in a significant difference in student achievement. Training staff on the difference between the two can be of great benefit to our students.

2. Innovative Practices are Created

Typically, when teachers/counselors learn about growth mindset, they give themselves permission to see their own potential for growth, and often attempt innovative ideas in their teaching.

3. Mistakes Are Modeled as Part of Learning

When educators stretch their brains and step out of their comfort zone, they can also model how mistakes and formative feedback can create better attempts next time. This will help students see what learning looks like through the lens of failing forward.

4. Educators Learn the Importance of Seeing Potential In All Students

If educators see students through a growth mindset lens, they begin to see more potential, and that creates positive change all around. Consider the studies that have been done regarding teacher preconceived notions of students.

Examine this study to clarify the last point on seeing potential in students. Imagine if you were a graduate student in a psychology class and you were given the task of working with a rat in a cage (I know, rats are different than students. But go with me here). If your professor asked you, "Do you think your thoughts could influence how this rat moves through space?", what would you say or think?

In a study like this, almost unanimously people said, “No, I can’t merely look at the rats and influence their performance,” thinking that would be an impossible superpower. The scientist who did this study, Bob Rosenthal (1963), proved that people could, in fact, look at a subject and affect their behavior, based on how they were viewed. Rats labeled “smart” did twice as well as those not labeled smart (www.npr.org/2015/01/23/379134306/batman-pt-1).

The rats that were in the cage labeled “smart” were treated and handled as smarter. Rosenthal’s other work on experimenter expectancy or the Pygmalion effect is another fascinating study. When one considers educators as the “experimenter” and the students as the “subjects,” we can suggest that if teachers think their students are able (regardless of historical performance) to learn and achieve (growth mindset) then this leads to the assumption that teachers who believe there is potential in their students will have students with better results.

Carol Dweck has looked further into how teachers viewed their students and how this could affect the students’ outcomes. As you guessed, teachers who saw potential in their students had students perform better. The implication of this research is important to examine. We “handle” students differently if we think they have potential. AND, if you have a growth mindset about students and understand that they can achieve tough goals even if they haven’t proven it yet, you will see better student outcomes. As educators, the words we use are powerful. Praising students’ effort instead of praising intelligence is a key part of supporting students adoption of a growth mindset. These growth mindset concepts are so important to intertwine into our school culture, which is why staff development as described in this chapter would benefit staff and thereby benefit students. As we come to see more and more research supporting growth mindset, it is apparent that teachers not only need to teach growth mindset, but model it. The following pages outline how this staff development can look.

SECTION ONE

Staff Professional Development (Grades K-8)

In this section, you will find a step-by-step guide for implementing Professional Development for the K-8 staff of your school. The reproducible documents, emails, PPT, and ideas in this section serve as planning resources and include the following:

- Flowchart: How to Set Up Growth Mindset Professional Development (Grades K-8)
- Pre-Training Email To Staff (Grades K-8)
- PPT Guide for Staff Development (Grades K-8)
- Discussion Questions Staff (Grades K-8)
- Follow-Up Email to Staff (Grades K-8)

Flowchart: How to Set Up Growth Mindset Professional Development
(Grades K-8)

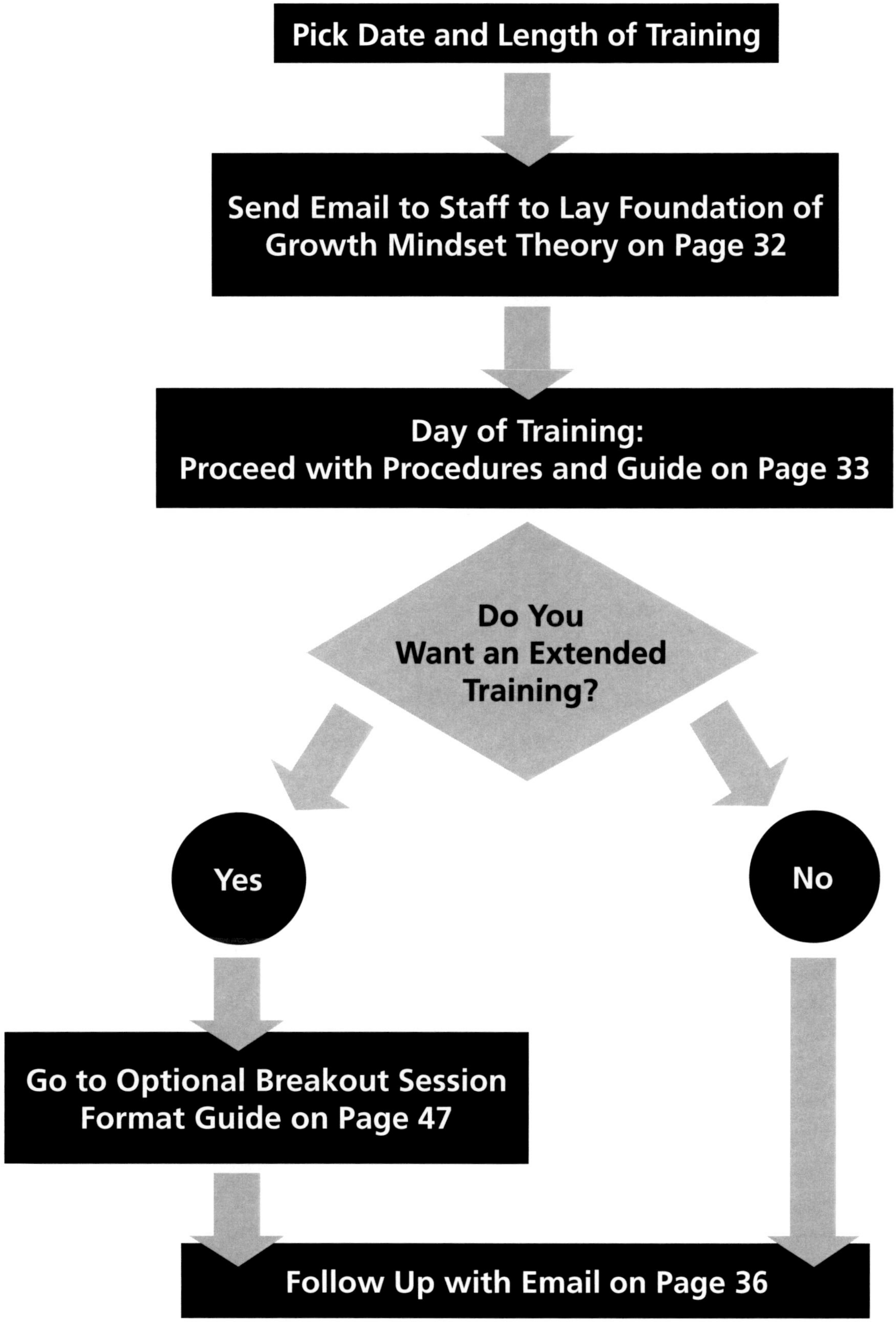

Pre-Training Email to Staff
(Grades K-8)

Prior to the staff development presentation, send this email so educators in your building have a foundation for the presentation.

To: Staff

Subject: Growth Mindset Staff Development

In preparation for our upcoming professional development on growth mindset, here are two videos you may be interested in watching. Both give helpful background knowledge that will serve as a springboard for our discussion.

1. This video explains Growth Mindset in an engaging way (8 minutes):
Trevor Ragan, *Growth Mindset Introduction: What it is, how it Works, and Why It Matters*

2. This is the TED Talk from Carol Dweck, pioneer of the growth mindset theory (11 minutes):
Carol Dweck: The Power of Believing You Can Improve

I think you will enjoy learning more about this exciting way to think differently, and I look forward to stretching our brains together!

Regards,

If someone performed medicine the same way as 30 years ago, it would be malpractice. Same for teaching.

– Alice Keeler

Download the PowerPoint file to guide you through this lesson at:
https://ncyi.org/integratingmindset

PPT What Is Growth Mindset: Creating a School Culture of Effort and Success

(See guide on pages 33-34 for specific script to lead training. Sample slides from PPT are below)

GUIDE FOR PPT for Grades K-8 Staff Development

Materials: PPT *from digital landing page noted above*

Duration: This PPT can last from 15-30 minutes

Preparation:

1. Several days prior to training, send the email from page 40 to staff, which includes videos links that will establish a foundation for growth mindset discussion.
2. Make copies of Discussion Questions and/or Staff Handout on page 35 and/or page 16.
3. Download PPT from digital landing page (https://ncyi.org/integratingmindset)

When you download the PPT, check out this icon which indicates a hyperlinked video explaining more about each term.

Slide # **What to do/say on that slide**

1. Introduce yourself and share that today we will be learning about growth mindset.
2. Ask the group by a show of hands how many know about growth mindset.
3. Growth mindset is a concept pioneered by Carol Dweck of Stanford University. This video clip will explain more of an overview (hyperlink is on this slide, and can be found on YouTube as *Growth Mindset: What it is, How It Works, and Why It Matters*).
4. Review the benefits of teaching students about growth mindset at a young age; similar to the benefits of learning musical instruments or foreign languages at a young age.

Continued on next page.

5. Why should educators learn about growth mindset? Research has shown that if teachers adopt a growth mindset, and believe that all students CAN learn (even despite past test scores/grades) then students will achieve better than if they were in class with a teacher who has a fixed mindset (this goes along with ideas of pre-conceived notions and self-fulfilling prophecies).

6. On this slide, we see an acrostic with the word MINDSET running alongside the left. Each topic in this acrostic designates a concept that is important in understanding growth mindset. Highlight the topics of Identifying Brain Basics (neuroplasticity, the ability for the brain to grow) and the power of yet, meaning that if someone doesn't understand something it is crucial to know, the person just doesn't know it YET. Helping students understand these concepts leads to better achievement. Ensuring educators understand this concept is equally important (direct staff to video links that will help them expand their knowledge at lisakingcounselor.com).

7. Show the visual of the buffet table and talk about how schools that roll out a growth mindset initiative start at different levels. We are sampling from the buffet by choosing to implement staff development pieces. In your individual classrooms, or collectively, we will come back and try things from the "buffet."

8. Three of the major concepts within growth mindset are: neuroplasticity, the power of yet, and grit.

9. One of the goals for today's session is for you to have some concrete ideas of what you can do to help students adopt a growth mindset. This video clip shows the importance of praising effort instead of intelligence. Watch this video clip that explains more about this research (video can be found on YouTube titled *Carol Dweck: A Study on Praise and Mindsets*).

10. Discuss how to reinforce growth mindset in your classrooms.

11. Research, both on the international level and in local schools, helps us show stakeholders how teaching growth mindset can influence achievement scores.

12. Give participants a moment to talk to someone next to them about ideas of how implementing growth mindset ideas might look in their classroom.

13. On a scale of 1-5, how much do you feel like you now know about growth mindset?

14. Thank you for stretching your brain with me today!

Extension: Have staff turn in answers to the discussion questions for a raffle. Prizes can be gift card or a jeans pass, an early out, extra planning time, etc.

Staff Discussion Questions
(Grades K-8)

Please answer these questions as we go through training.

1. What is the difference between growth mindset and fixed mindset?

2. Why is it important for students to learn about growth mindset and the power of yet?

3. What is the benefit of teachers adopting a growth mindset?

4. How do you think you can incorporate growth mindset concepts into your program/ classroom?

Follow Up Email to Staff
(Grades K-8)

Below is an email that can be sent to staff after delivering a staff training. This email will reiterate some of the main points of training and also provide addition resources to those who might be interested.

Hello Fellow Staff,

I wanted to follow up on our professional development on growth mindset. I hope you learned a few things that provide fresh insight and inspiration. One of the main things I took away is the need for us to try new things, EVEN IF THEY DON'T WORK. This gives us an opportunity to explain to students how we try new things, and ask for feedback so we can continually work to make things better. This can also be valuable for students as they strive to get better, one step at a time. I look forward to seeing our school filled with programs that integrate the power of yet, the importance of grit, and the process of neuroplasticity, and am glad to walk this journey of learning with you!

If you are interested in more information about growth mindset, see this website for books, articles and videos that will help stretch your brain.

http://bit.ly/2slHYPb

Regards,

CHAPTER TWO

2

SECTION TWO

Staff Professional Development (Grades 9-12)

In this section, you will find a step-by-step guide for implementing Professional Development for 9-12 staff of your school. The reproducible documents, emails, PPT, and ideas in this section serve as planning resources and include the following:

- Flowchart: How to Set Up Growth Mindset Professional Development (Grades 9-12)
- Pre-Training Email to Staff (Grades 9-12)
- Discussion Questions to Staff (Grades 9-12)
- Follow-Up Email to Staff (Grades 9-12)
- Handout for Staff (Grades 9-12)

Flowchart: How to Set Up Growth Mindset Professional Development
(Grades 9-12)

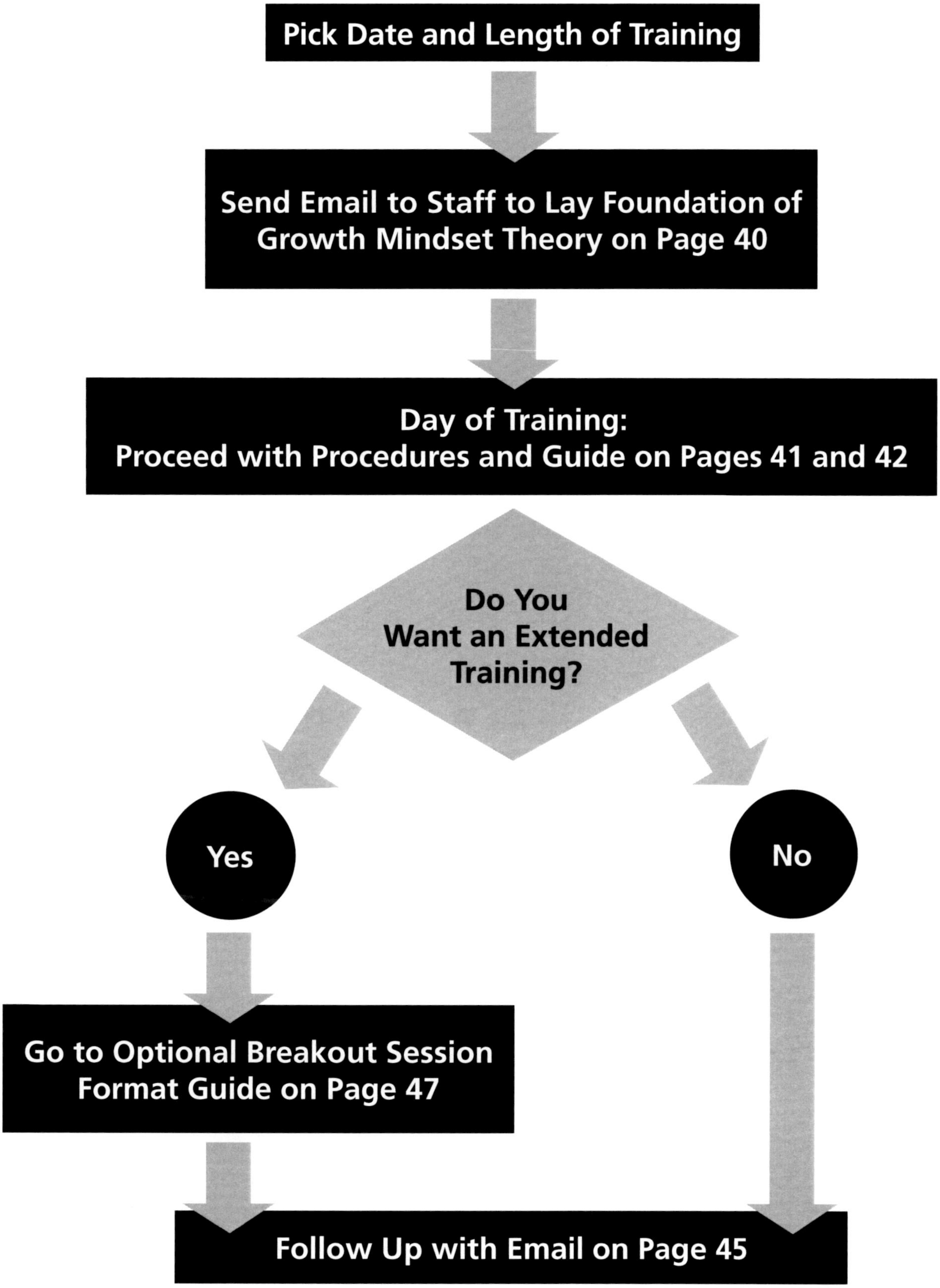

Pre-Training Email to Staff

(Grades 9-12)

Prior to the staff development presentation, send this email so educators in your building have a foundation for the presentation.

To: Staff

Re: Growth Mindset Staff Development

This email is to help ensure you have foundational information on the background of growth mindset theory prior to our upcoming training. In a national study by *Education Week*, 85% of educators said they wanted more training on this very topic, and we are excited to provide it.

Please watch the brief video noted below, prior to our session. This will give you background and research information as we begin to dig deeper into a concept that can create a culture of success and grit in our school.

We will be exploring growth mindset further as the year goes on and I look forward to learning important new information about this powerful research-based theory along with you.

Video: Trevor Ragan, *Growth Mindset Introduction: What it is, How it Works, and Why It Matters*

Sincerely,

Continuous effort–not strength or intelligence–is the key to unlocking our potential.

– Winston S. Churchill

Download the PowerPoint file to guide you through this lesson at:
https://ncyi.org/integratingmindset

PPT What is Growth Mindset: Creating a School Culture of Effort and Success

(See guide on pages 41 and 42 for specific script to lead training. Sample slides from PPT are below)

GUIDE FOR PPT for Grades 9-12 Staff Development

Materials: PPT *from digital landing page noted above*

Duration: This PPT can last from 15-30 minutes

Preparation:

1. Several days prior to training, send the email from page 40 to staff, which includes videos links that will establish a foundation for growth mindset discussion.
2. Make copies of Staff Discussion Questions and/or Staff Handout on page 44 and/or page 17.
3. Download PPT from digital landing page (https://ncyi.org/integratingmindset)

When you download the PPT, check out this icon which indicates a hyperlinked video explaining more about each term.

Slide # **What to do/say on that slide**

1. Introduce yourself and share that today we will be learning about growth mindset.
2. Ask the group by a show of hands how many know about growth mindset.
3. Growth mindset is a concept pioneered by Carol Dweck of Stanford University. This video clip will explain more of an overview (hyperlink is on this slide, and can be found on YouTube as *Growth Mindset: What it is, How It Works, and Why It Matters*).
4. Review the benefits of teaching students about growth mindset at a young age; similar to the benefits of learning musical instruments or foreign languages at a young age.

Continued on next page.

5. Why should educators learn about growth mindset? Research has shown that if teachers adopt a growth mindset, and believe that all students CAN learn (even despite past test scores/grades) then, students will achieve more than if they were in class with a teacher who has a fixed mindset (this goes along with ideas of pre-conceived notions and self-fulfilling prophecies).

6. On this slide, we see an acrostic with the word MINDSET running alongside the left. Each topic in this acrostic designates a concept that is important in understanding growth mindset. Highlight the topics of Identifying Brain Basics (neuroplasticity, the ability for the brain to grow) and the power of yet, meaning that if someone doesn't understand something it is crucial to know, the person just doesn't know it YET. Helping students understand these concepts leads to better achievement. Ensuring educators understand this concept is equally important (direct staff to video links that will help them expand their knowledge at lisakingcounselor.com).

7. Show the visual of the buffet table and talk about how schools that roll out a growth mindset initiative start at different levels. We are sampling from the buffet by choosing to implement staff development pieces. In your individual classrooms, or collectively, we will come back and try things from the "buffet."

8. Three of the major concepts within growth mindset are: neuroplasticity, the power of yet, and grit.

9. One of the goals for today's session is for you to have some concrete ideas of what you can do to help students adopt a growth mindset. This video clip shows the importance of praising effort instead of intelligence. Watch this video clip that explains more about this research (video can be found on YouTube titled *Carol Dweck: A Study on Praise and Mindsets*).

10. Discuss how to reinforce growth mindset in your classrooms.

11. Research, both on the international level and in local schools, helps us show stakeholders how teaching growth mindset can influence achievement scores.

12. Give participants a moment to talk to someone next to them about ideas of how implementing growth mindset ideas might look in their classroom.

13. On a scale of 1-5, how much do you feel like you now know about growth mindset?

14. Thank you for stretching your brain with me today!

Extension: Have staff turn in answers to the discussion questions for a raffle. Prizes can be gift card or a jeans pass, an early out, extra planning time, etc.

Download the PowerPoint file to guide you through this lesson at:
https://ncyi.org/integratingmindset

PPT What is Growth Mindset: Creating a School Culture of Effort and Success

(See guide on pages 41 and 42 for specific script to lead training. Sample slides from PPT are below)

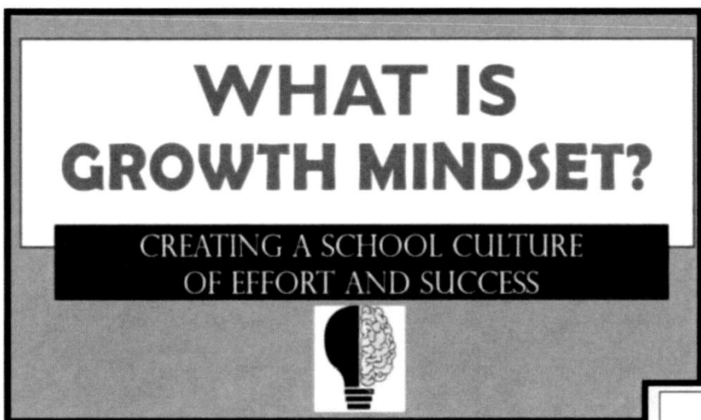

Download this PPT, tweak it for your needs, and run a brief professional development session that will benefit your staff.

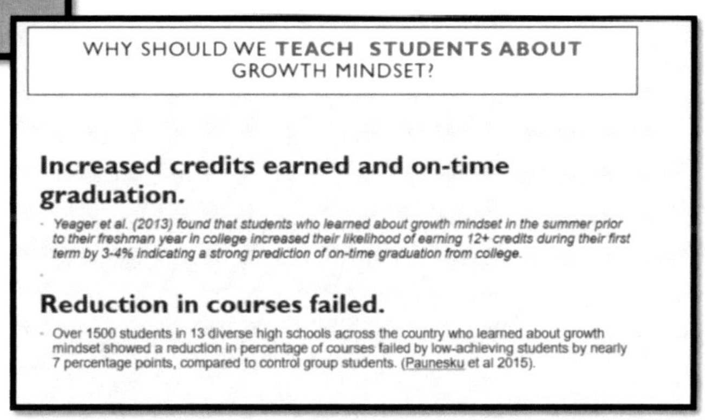

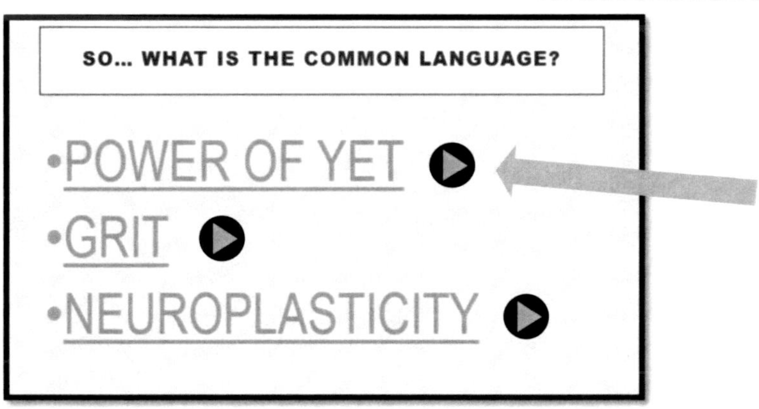

When you download the PPT, check out this icon which indicates there is a hyperlinked video that will explain more about each term.

Staff Discussion Questions
(Grades 9-12)

Please answer these questions as we go through training.

1. How would you briefly summarize what it means to have a growth mindset?

2. A 2015 study (Paunesku et al.) showed that implementing a lesson on growth mindset as an intervention helped raise the GPA among high school students at risk for dropping out of school. **How do you think we could do an intervention here to address our at-risk or underperforming students?**

3. How can you incorporate these concepts of growth mindset in the ways you relate to your students:

- The Power of Yet:
- Grit:
- Neuroplasticity:

4. How can having a growth mindset help with these career readiness skills?

- Complex Problem Solving
- Critical Thinking
- Creativity
- People Management
- Coordinationg with Others
- Emotional Intelligence
- Judgment and Decision Making
- Service Orientation
- Negotiation
- Cognitive Flexibility

Source: *Top 10 Career Readiness Skills*, Future of Jobs Report, World Economic Forum

Follow Up Email to Staff
(Grades 9-12)

After completing training on growth mindset, follow up with staff to provide them with additional resources and the opportunity to reflect on what they learned.

To: Staff

Re: Follow-Up on Growth Mindset Training

I hope you found the growth mindset training worthwhile. We know from recent studies that 75% of students with a growth mindset also had GPA scores that improved over time. The practices we implement in our classrooms can be simple, but encouraging students to adopt a growth mindset is an important part of the process. We welcome any thoughts you have on the training and wanted to pass along a few other resources you might enjoy:

Angela Duckworth's book GRIT
GRIT by Angela Duckworth l Animated CORE Message

Resource page with helpful articles and videos
Growth Mindset Resources at www.lisakingcounselor.com

Quick overview of neuroplasticity:
Neuroplasticity

Interesting podcast on Grit (about 45 minutes long)
How to Get More Grit in Your Life - Freakonomics

Breakout Session Format Option

Recently, upon finishing the second year of *Mindset Matters* curriculum at our school, I had the pleasure of sitting with my principal to brainstorm about growth mindset staff development for the next year. I say it was a pleasure because I am fortunate to work for a gifted leader who is supportive of all things that will benefit students. She says "yes" to any request that is feasible and worthwhile, and works hard to help bring others' visions to life. My principal, Missy Shackelford, is a walking growth mindset.

Her open-mindedness led to a conversation on how to build on our growth mindset culture. The conversation went something like this:

Me: "I would love to put a date on the calendar to do a growth mindset training."

Missy, my principal: "Sounds great, what are you thinking?"

Me: "What do you think about a 30-minute session where I cover the basics of research showing how growth mindset benefits students, and then talk through best practices for implementation?"

Principal: "Why don't we use one of our staff development days and do it a bit differently? I don't want any of us to think growth mindset is something only discussed during counseling lessons. I want our staff to hear about aspects of growth mindset from different people so they know I expect growth mindset to be going on all the time."

(Thought in my head: WIN!!! Jaw drop).

Me: "That is awesome!"

Principal: "What if we do a full staff mini-session of about 15 minutes on growth mindset and then let staff choose a breakout session to attend afterwards? We can have one led by the gifted teacher, one by admin, one by the counselors, and one by a teacher who has been teaching growth mindset concepts in their class. That way, growth mindset is for all of us and presented by all of us."

(This is how the breakout session format on page 47 was created).

Principal Missy Shackelford says...

"I don't want the staff to think growth mindset is something you only do during counseling lessons. I want the staff to hear different aspects of it from different school leaders so they know I expect growth mindset to be going on all the time."

Growth Mindset Staff Development Breakout Session Format

"What is Growth Mindset?" Mini-Session (Duration: 15-30 minutes)

See pages 41-42 for overview and link to PPT

If you want to extend the day of learning, staff can choose which breakout session to attend. According to time limits of the professional development, staff could rotate to 1,2, or more of these sessions.

- **How Trauma Affects the Brain and Basic Neuroscience**
- **Helping the Perfectionists with Growth Mindset**
- **Grit...What Is It? And How Can I Reinforce It in My Classroom?**
- **Mindfulness**

Possible presenters for breakout sessions can be teachers, counselors, administrators, school social workers/psychologists, or guest speakers.

Breakout sessions can be tweaked according to school needs and availability of breakout session leaders.

Use the survey on page 48 to learn more about your staff needs and preferences.

Needs Assessment For Breakout Sessions

Directions: Staff, please read through the ideas below and let us know what topics you find most interesting as we plan our upcoming staff development.

Check off the three topics you want to learn more about:

___How Trauma Affects the Brain and Basic Neuroscience

___Helping Perfectionists Deal with Failure by Learning about Growth Mindset

___Grit... What Is It? And How Can I Reinforce It In My Classroom?

___Testing, Assessment, and Growth Mindset

___Mindfulness

___College and Career Readiness and Growth Mindset

___The Research Behind Math and Growth Mindset

Videos and Articles that Can Be Used for Breakout Sessions

If someone leading a breakout session wants to add a supplemental video on their topic, see below for some great ideas.

TOPIC	URL	DURATION
How Trauma Affects the Brain and Basic Neuroscience		
How Childhood Trauma Affects Health Across a Lifetime	https://ed.ted.com/on/iOyQVfhd	15:59
After Watching, Your Brain will Never be the Same	https://www.youtube.com/watch?v=LNHBMFCzznE	14:24
Helping Perfectionists with Growth Mindset		
Perfectionism and Being Judgmental	https://www.innereffort.com/009-paul-colaianni-overwhelmed-brain-perfectionism-judgmental/	55:00
A Recovering Perfectionist's Journey to Give Up Grades	https://www.youtube.com/watch?v=_61kL5jeKqM	11:32
Grit...What is It? And How Can I Reinforce It in My Classroom?		
CORE message from Angela Duckworth's book GRIT	https://www.youtube.com/watch?v=sWctLEdlgi4	6:17
Using Grit to Succeed in School	https://www.youtube.com/watch?v=ZoYDHUGlwuE	2:00
Testing, Assessment and Growth Mindset		
The Power of Belief–Mindset and Success	https://www.youtube.com/watch?v=pN34FNbOKXc	10:52
Boosting Math	https://www.youtube.com/watch?v=ZoYDHUGlwuE&t=48s	8:51
Mindfulness		
Mindfulness and Neuroplasticity	https://www.youtube.com/watch?v=7TN23YiGkAQ	3:50
Why Aren't We Teaching You Mindfulness?	https://www.youtube.com/watch?v=-yJPcdiLEkI&t=329s	14:26
College and Career Readiness and Growth Mindset		
Grit, Mindset at Lonestar College, capabilities and career readiness	https://www.youtube.com/watch?v=SomhhosDw8U	4:15

Book Study

Book studies can be done in many ways. Options for book studies include:

- Encouraging staff to read one of the following books over the summer.
- Read one of these books throughout the year and have periodic meetings to review chapters.
- Have different teams be responsible for specific chapters and then have each team share their chapter with the whole group.

Book Title Ideas for Book Studies:

CHAPTER THREE

3

Easy-To-Implement Parent Workshops on Growth Mindset

The Importance of Parent Workshops

A key component to infusing a concept into your school community is to get the families involved. Offering a parent workshop is not only worthwhile in helping to keep parents informed on your initiatives, but also gives parents an opportunity to show they want to be involved at school. While some educators find doing a parent workshop can be intimidating, it is a display of your own growth mindset to step out of your comfort zone and offer a family night of learning. This chapter should make it easier, by giving step-by-step instructions on how to implement a parent workshop, including PPTs with video clips, handouts, and ideas to explore.

What things can you do to make a parent night successful?

* Mandatory for Success: Advertise

Optional:

- Create an opportunity for student involvement and provide child care
- Provide snacks
- Set up a photo booth
- Have someone capture photos at the event to use in follow-up emails, etc.
- Ask for volunteers to help, based on number of RSVPs
- Do a raffle for door prizes

> *I liked hearing the science behind the positive brain growth. I found it most interesting to hear children with a growth mindset would take on difficult tasks, rather than the easy ones. My biggest take-away was learning new ways to encourage my kids in education and life situations.*
>
> **Parent, after attending Growth Mindset Night**

SECTION ONE

Parent Workshop Ideas (Grades K-8)

In this section, you will find time lines, scripts, and tips for creating a Parent Night at your school. In the pages that follow, you will see two options for Grades K-8: a workshop with students present and one workshop for parents only.

- Flyer to Publicize Parent Night
- Parent Handouts
- Photo Booth
- Timeline, Planning, and PPT for Growth Mindset Night with Students
- Timeline, Planning, and PPT for Growth Mindset Parents-Only Workshop
- Follow Up Email
- Parent Workshop Survey

Parent Workshop Ideas
(Grades K-8)

One way to infuse growth mindset into your school community is by educating the parents. Recently, I attended a school council meeting where they were deciding whether or not to bring growth mindset in as a school-wide initiative. One father brought up the point that we need to sell the parent workshop to families based on the "why," not necessarily the "what." He used his sales/ marketing expertise to remind us that parents want to know about programs that help their kids deal with overcoming adversity as they work through inevitable struggles in their journey towards graduation and beyond. Remember to sell the "why" when setting up one of the following options:

OPTION A
Growth Mindset Night

This option consists of a parent workshop with students attending a childcare /movie simultaneously. For the last 15 minutes of the program, the students join the parents for an activity and growth mindset discussion.

-or-

OPTION B
A Parents-Only Workshop

Same workshop, but childcare is not provided.

Use the ideas in this section to create what works best for your community. Think outside the box and make changes. Consider inviting neighboring schools and/or feeder pattern schools.

Growth Mindset Night

A night for families to learn about growth mindset.
Your kids are learning it and we want you to know about it, too!

When: ______________________________

Time: ______________________________

Where: ______________________________

I Will Attend Growth Mindset Night!

Please return this to your child's teacher by ________.

# of adults: ______________________________

adults names attending: ______________________________

____

email of adults attending: ______________________________

____

# of school-aged kids attending: ______________________________

Parent's Handout 1.1

What is Growth Mindset?

A Growth Mindset is an understanding that intelligence can grow, and with hard work and positive thinking, obstacles can be overcome.

Tips to Help!

TIP #1

If you hear your child say, "I can't" or "I don't get it!" have them add YET to the end of the sentence. "I can't do it YET" or "I don't get it YET!"

TIP #2

Have conversations with your kids that it's OK to fail as long as they learn from those failures/mistakes.

TIP #3

Read books to your child like *The Little Engine that Could*; *Amazing Grace*; *Leo the Late Bloomer*; *Everyone Can Learn to Ride a Bicycle*; and *What to Do with a Problem*.

TIP #4

Praise the effort of your child. Research has shown us that saying, "You are working really hard on that!" is more beneficial than telling a child, "You are so smart." Praising effort makes kids want to try-hard even if they are unsure of themselves.

Want to Learn More about Growth Mindset?

Watch

What?

A TED Talk by the pioneer of Growth Mindset, Carol Dweck, is 10 minutes and really interesting.

Where Can I Find It?

Search on www.TED.com: *Carol Dweck, The Power of Believing that You Can Improve*.

https://www.ted.com/talks/carol_dweck_the_power_of_believing_that_you_can_improve

---

What?

An eight-minute video that is a great overview explaining what Growth Mindset is and some of the research backing up the benefits.

Where Can I Find It?

Search on www.YouTube.com: Growth Mindset Introduction: What It Is, How It Works, and Why It Matters.

https://www.youtube.com/watch?v=75GFzikmRYO

Read

Mindsets for Parents Strategies to Encourage Growth Mindsets in Kids
by Mary Cay Ricci

The Gift of Failure
by Jessica Lahey

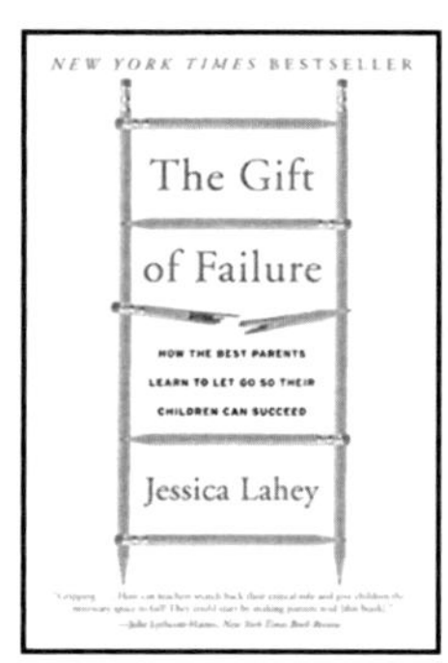

Article: *Developing A Growth Mindset – 5 Tips for Parents* (June 2015)
https://www.oxfordlearning.com/growth-mindset-tips-for-parents/

Growth Mindset Discussion Questions

1. What can you say to yourself if you don't understand something and you are feeling like you will never get it right?
2. Who is one person you notice is very hard working?
3. What is one skill you are interested in getting better at? How can you make sure you improve at that skill (give details about your plan)?

Staircase of Learning

Which step are you on?

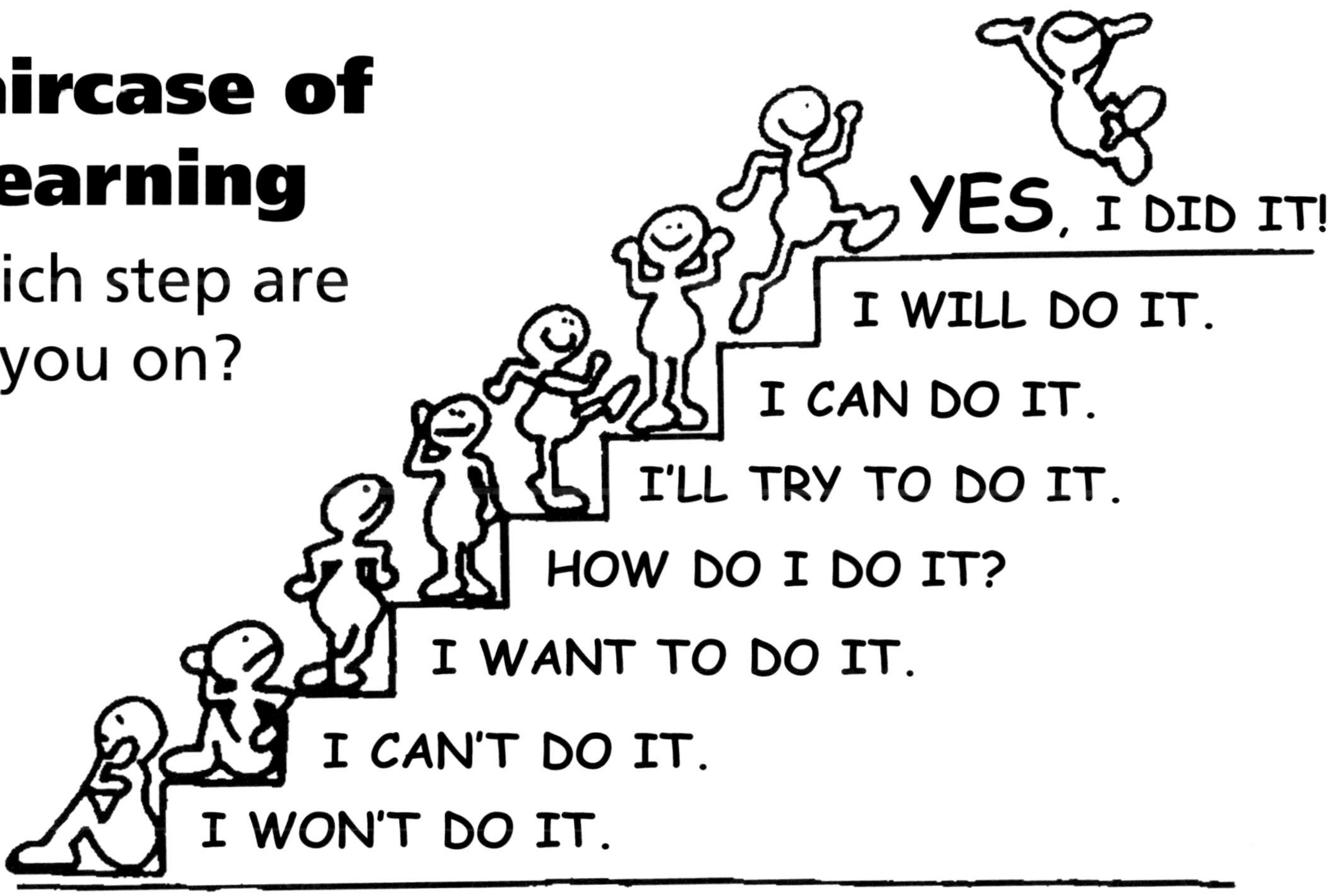

Photo Booth for the Night of the Event

One idea for creating a night of learning engagement combined with fun, is to set up a photo booth. The idea is to create memories for families. Having someone from your team available to capture images of the night will also serve as a way to give positive visual reminders of a fun night in your follow-up emails, social media, etc.

What you will need?

- Photo booth accessories (available at many party stores): fun hats, scarfs, glasses, signs, etc.
- Make your own signs or use speech bubbles glued onto poster board, card stock, or sturdy cardboard (you might even want to write the phrases larger).

Option: Hang a curtain on the wall with a poster saying " I BELIEVE IN MY SELFIE."

Let parents, families, kids, and staff have fun at the selfie booth! You can set this up so families that arrive early can snap pics before the session begins, and you can remind families at the end of the workshop (our booth had a line out the door after our presentation!).

Option A: Timeline and Planning for Parent Workshops with Students Invited
(Grades K-8)

Advance Preparation:

_____ Put a date on the school's master calendar for Growth Mindset Night (this can be done in planning for the year or a few months ahead of the event).

_____Get volunteers for monitoring students who will be watching a movie during part of the parent workshop (if you're using Option A).

_____ One to three weeks before the event, send home the Parent Flyer (Page 58)

_____ Starting one week prior to the event, do a "shout out" on afternoon announcements, and send a email blast or newsletter to all parents about the upcoming family night.

> Sample Afternoon Announcement
>
> **GROWTH MINDSET NIGHT IS COMING UP NEXT WEEK!**
>
> Many of you have been learning about Growth Mindset and how to train your brain. Now it's time for your parents to come learn about growth mindset, too!
>
> Flyers went home yesterday, so remind your parents to return an RSVP so we can get a headcount for our ________(date) Growth Mindset Night here at ______________(school).

Workshop Night Preparations:

_____ Make copies of parent handout. If you want to conserve paper, you can make it double sided on half sheets. (page 61)

_____ Make copies of parent survey (page 67)

_____ Choose appropriate movie and a good room in which to have the students watch the movie

_____ Make copies of discussion question (page 59) with "What Step Have You Reached Today?" on the front and Discussion Questions on the back

_____ Buy pipe cleaners and gallon Ziploc bags in bulk

_____ Divide 10 pipe cleaners into each Ziploc bag depending on number of RSVP's

For PPT presentation

____ Download PPT

____ Follow guide on pages 62 and 63

Download the PowerPoint file to guide you through this lesson at:
https://ncyi.org/integratingmindset

Option A:
GUIDE FOR PPT for Parent Workshop With Students
(Grades K-8)

Materials: PPT *from digital landing page noted above*

Duration: This PPT can last approximately 30 minutes

Preparation: Download PPT from website

Slide #	What to do/say on that slide
1.	(Slide to have up when people enter).
2.	Welcome to Growth Mindset night. Ask what grades everyone's children are in, "Raise your hand if you have a kindergartener. If you have a 1st grader?" Etc.
3.	Review the agenda for the evening.
4.	Explain the difference between growth mindset and fixed mindset.
5.	Share info about the vast research supporting when growth mindset is taught, positive outcomes occur in academic and social/emotional responses.
6.	Watch videos: Carol Dweck giving background about growth mindset and how Khan Academy uses growth mindset research.
7.	Invite parents to think about which mindset they would rather their children have?
8.	Look at the difference in brain activity of fixed mindset vs. growth mindset brains.
9.	Give an overview of the curriculum that is being taught to our students.
10.	Explain that one thing being taught in the curriculum is a basic understanding of brain science. Review the "hand model" of the brain. Note: If you, as presenter, want an overview to brush up on this watch Lori Cross's YouTube video on the brain model https://www.youtube.com/watch?v=UNqTviVilH0.
11.	Expand on the brain science by describing the concept of "flipping your lid." Note: Read more about this explanation by reading article…*How to Teach Kids About the Brain: Laying Strong Foundations for Emotional Intelligence* at www.heysigmund.com.
12.	Read quote by Daniel Coyle about learning about the brain.
13.	Describe the learning process and the concept that when you don't know something you are in the "Not Yet" of learning.
14.	Play game as described on page 152 "I'm Going to the Moon" to highlight this concept.

15. Share how "The Stairway of Learning" is a good way to think about our attitude about learning. Ask participants to think about which stair they were on for the game we just played. This stairway is good to use with kids when they need to assess their level of motivation.
16. Review the concept of Grit and give reference to Angela Duckworth, PhD. Note: for review, refer to YouTube core message of the book at: https://www.youtube.com/watch?v=sWctLEdIgi4.
17. Schools can document interventions with growth mindset and locally take data on student achievement outcomes. Here, we see that the number of proficient readers increased significantly !
18. Look at this piece of research. The fact that so much research supports the benefits of growth mindset leads us to ask "Why wouldn't we teach about growth mindset to parents? And teachers? And students?"
19. Watch video of the research that has supported the praise of effort vs. the praise of intelligence (video from YouTube https://www.youtube.com/watch?v=NWv1VdDeoRY).
20. Give ideas for what parents can say with "Instead of this, Say this."
21. Introduce three ways to encourage your child to have a growth mindset (praising effort, modeling in our own behavior, and acknowledging others who display a growth mindset).
22. Preview what is coming up when the kids come in.
23. While the kids are returning from their activity, have parents discuss one thing they learned.
24. When the kids return into the room, gather everyone together to do the mindset chant, teaching the kids and the parents this multisensory way to learn about growth mindset.
25. Introduce video for kids and parents to understand brains better (video is hyperlinked: *Ned the Neuron* on YouTube by Kizoom).
26. Tell parents "We are going to have the kids do an activity that will give you the opportunity to praise their effort." Introduce the Pipe Cleaner Challenge on page 154. Allow families to spread out across the room.
27. Call families back together, review the The Stairway of Learning, and ask children to think about what step they were on in this game. Ask kids what step they are on when they are doing difficult math? Playing a sport? Cleaning their room?
28. End the session with a big cheer all together (kids and parents), "Whatcha Got to Do? You've Got to Train Your Brain! Hopefully tonight gave you insight into new ideas, but if you feel like you don't get growth mindset, remember that you just don't get it…YET!"
29. Remind families to visit the photo booth.
30. Ask if there are any questions and thank everyone for coming. Stay around for questions.

Option: Encourage parents to take the handout home and discuss it with their kids. The Stairway of Learning is great to hang up on the refrigerator!

Download the PowerPoint file to guide you through this lesson at: **https://ncyi.org/integratingmindset**

Option B:
GUIDE FOR PPT for Parent Workshop – Parents Only
(Grades K-8)

Materials: PPT *from digital landing page noted above*

Duration: This PPT can last approximately 30 minutes

Preparation: Download PPT from website.

Slide # **What to do/say on that slide**

1. (Slide to have up when people enter).
2. Welcome to Growth Mindset night. Ask what grades everyone's children are in, "Raise your hand if you have a kindergartener. If you have a 1st grader?" Etc.
3. Ask parents… to start off our discussion about intelligence and doing well in school, let me ask you this question. "How much success comes from talent and how much is effort? What percentages would you say?"
4. Explain the difference between growth mindset and fixed mindset.
5. Share info about the vast research supporting when growth mindset is taught, positive outcomes occur in academic and social/emotional responses.
6. Watch videos: Carol Dweck giving background about growth mindset and how Khan Academy uses growth mindset research.
7. Invite parents to think about which mindset they would rather their children have?
8. Look at the difference in brain activity of fixed mindset vs. growth mindset brains.
9. Give an overview of the curriculum that is being taught to our students.
10. Explain that one thing being taught in the curriculum is a basic understanding of brain science. Review the "hand model" of the brain. Note: If you, as presenter, want an overview to brush up on this watch Lori Cross's YouTube video on the brain model https://www.youtube.com/watch?v=UNqTviVilH0.
11. Expand on the brain science by describing the concept of "flipping your lid." Note: Read more about this explanation by reading article…*How to Teach Kids About the Brain: Laying Strong Foundations for Emotional Intelligence* at www.heysigmund.com.

12. Read quote by Daniel Coyle about learning about the brain.
13. Describe the learning process and concept that when you don't know something you are in the "Not Yet" of learning.
14. Play game as described on page 152 "I'm Going to the Moon" to highlight this concept.
15. Review the concept of Grit and give reference to Angela Duckworth, PhD. This characteristic has been found to be a common trait among the most successful people in a number of different domains such as: athletics, executive leadership, the armed forces, etc. Note: for review, refer to YouTube core message of the book at: https://www.youtube.com/watch?v=sWctLEdIgi4.
16. Many local schools, which have implemented growth mindset initiatives, have documented how these interventions have impacted local test scores. Here, we see a graph showing that reading proficiency increased significantly after participating in a growth mindset curriculum.
17. Look at this piece of research. The fact that so much research supports the benefits of growth mindset leads us to ask "Why wouldn't we teach about growth mindset to parents? And teachers? And students?"
18. Watch video of the research that has supported the praise of effort vs. the praise of intelligence (on YouTube at https://www.youtube.com/watch?v=NWv1VdDeoRY).
19. Give ideas for what parents can say with "Instead of this, say this."
20. Introduce three ways to encourage your child to have a growth mindset (praising effort, modeling in our own behavior, and acknowledging others who display a growth mindset).
21. Have parents share which idea they plan to try with their children to encourage a growth mindset.
22. Review the The Stairway of Learning and ask about what step they were on in this game. Ask what step they think their kids are on when they are doing difficult math? Playing a sport? Cleaning their room?
23. End the session with a reminder of what the students will be learning by asking, "Whatcha Got to Do? You've Got to Train Your Brain! Hopefully tonight gave you insight into new ideas, but if you feel like you don't get growth mindset, remember that you just don't get it…YET!"
24. Ask if there are any questions and thank parents for coming. Stay around for questions.

Option: Encourage parents to take the handout home and discuss it with their kids. The Stairway of Learning is great to hang up on the refrigerator!

Follow Up Email for Parents

If you ask for parents to give their email address on the RSVP, you can send a thank you/follow up email like the one below; even the ones who wanted to attend, but couldn't.

Dear Parents,

Thank you for your interest in Growth Mindset Night! We had a great turn out and appreciate your commitment to being an advocate for your child's success. As one of the attendees pointed out...having a growth mindset is not always easy. How true! It takes practice to help our kids (and ourselves) use these new skills and ideas.

We would love to get your feedback on the evening so we know what your favorite parts were and how we can make it even better in the future (after all, we want to stretch our brains and always be improving our skills too)! Attached is a survey you can complete and return.

It was a pleasure being with you. Please let us know if you have further questions. Also, here's a website resource, if you are interested in learning more about growth mindset. http://lisakingcounselor.com/index.php/growth-mindset-resources/.

Name

Title, School

More communication with parents = better relationships

The following email came from a parent who couldn't attend the session but received the follow-up email and asked for the handouts.

> ***"Thank you so much for sending me the information from the Growth Mindset workshop. I had an opportunity to view the videos today. I am speechless (and if you knew me, you would know that doesn't happen too often. LOL). I will definitely start working on developing my growth mindset. Thanks, again."***

Parent Growth Mindset Workshop Survey

Excellent = 4   Good = 3   Fair = 2   Not Yet = 1

1. Presentation:

4   3   2   1

2. Handout(s):

4   3   2   1

3. Video Clips:

4   3   2   1

4. Kids Activity (If Applicable):

4   3   2   1

5. Overall:

4   3   2   1

6. Were the activities during the workshop useful? Why, or why not?

____

____

7. What were the most helpful aspects of the program?

____

____

8. What can be improved?

____

____

9. Would you recommend this workshop to another parent? ❑ Yes ❑ No
Why, or why not?

____

____

10. Any other feedback or comments?

____

____

SECTION TWO

Parent Workshop Ideas (Grades 9-12)

In this section you will see a script for a Parent Workshop that will guide you through the PPT provided. There is a timeline, tips, and handouts that will help you put together a seamless program for parents.

- Flyer to Publicize Parent Night
- Parent Quiz
- Parent Handout
- Timeline, Planning, and PPT for Growth Mindset Parent Workshop
- Parent Workshop Survey

Workshop Ideas in a High School Setting

US News & World Report columnist Laura McMullen writes about the fact that as students get older, their parents tend to get more disengaged (ie, going to less PTA meetings, school events, etc). She adds that the data also shows parental involvement in school correlates with higher GPA's in high school. Clearly, these facts lead to a quandary. If parent involvement correlates with higher grades, how can we create events that will keep the parents involved in the secondary grades? (US News and World Report, Feb 20, 2012)

As a way to begin implementing parent workshops, try inviting parents to participate in:

- Parents Book Club (*Mindset for Parents* by Mary Cay Ricci, among other books that are on page 50)
- Lunch & Learn sessions on different topics
- Presentation at a PTA meeting or Open House Night
- Parent Workshop for Unmotivated Students
- Parent Workshop for College Bound Students
- Parent Workshop with Students Also Attending Session

Think about what type of parent workshop would work best for your school's population.

Decide on a topic, and schedule a date on the calendar. If you don't plan it, it will be just a wish.

Growth Mindset Parent Workshop

Are you wondering:

- How to help your child make better grades?
- How to get your child motivated?
- What techniques to use with your child who gets easily frustrated?
- How to encourage your child who gives up quickly?
- How to help foster independence in your child?

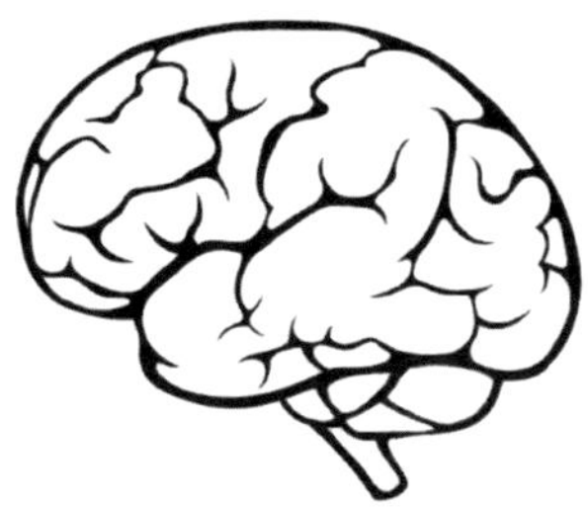

Topic of Discussion

TRAINING YOUR BRAIN: THE SCIENCE BEHIND A GROWTH MINDSET

Childcare, Door Prizes, and Refreshments Provided

Please fill out and return to your child's teacher if you are interested in attending.

Parent Name ______________________ Phone ______________________

Child's Name ______________________ Homeroom ______________________

Number of Children Who Will Need Childcare ______________________

Email Address ____

Parent Quiz

Part I.

Success is based on talent and effort. If you had to guess what percentage of each contributes to success, what would you say?

__________________ % effort + ____________________ % talent = SUCCESS

Part II.

Think about the following questions and choose the answer that best describes you.

1. Imagine that your child has always been a great soccer player. How would you react if your child came home and told you that he/she didn't make the soccer team?

A. I would be disappointed that my child didn't try his/her best.

B. I would call the coach and explain that my child had a bad day and needed another chance to tryout again.

C. I would be empathetic to my child's feelings and try to talk to my child about what he/she could do differently next time to make it a more successful tryout.

2. Your child shows you a math test that he/she got a 95 on. What are your first thoughts?

A. That kid is so smart and truly amazes me!

B. Awesome. My child's hard work has paid off.

C. I wonder how the other students in the class did on the test?

3. You hear that your child has Mr. Jackson, a teacher known for being harsh with students. You think:

A. I need to call and have his/her class changed.

B. Maybe he will be a good teacher for my child.

C. My child is going to be miserable!

Reflection: Which of the above reactions/thoughts are from a growth mindset? Which ones are from a fixed mindset?

> ***How good you are at something, is not an indicator of what you can become.***
>
> – Astronaut Mark Kelly

What is growth mindset?

Growth Mindset refers to the belief that intelligence can grow and we can actually get smarter with effort and hard work.

Why is it important for parents to know about growth mindset?

Having a growth mindset has been linked to being able to bounce back from failure. As astronaut Mark Kelly said, "How good you are is not an indicator of what you can become." Kids will try new skills and it will take many repetitions of that skill to master it. What we need to help our children understand is that it is up to THEM. How diligently they decide to practice will determine their eventual proficiency.

How does teaching our kids about growth mindset differ from telling them to "try harder?"

The difference with teaching growth mindset is in explaining the science behind ***effort***.

Practice leads to success. Pathways in our brain actually grow when we repeat a skill over and over. This repetitive effort builds a "memory" that ultimately moves us toward successfully achieving a skill. Telling our students (or ourselves) to "try harder" doesn't work. In reality, the better phrase is "do it again and again."

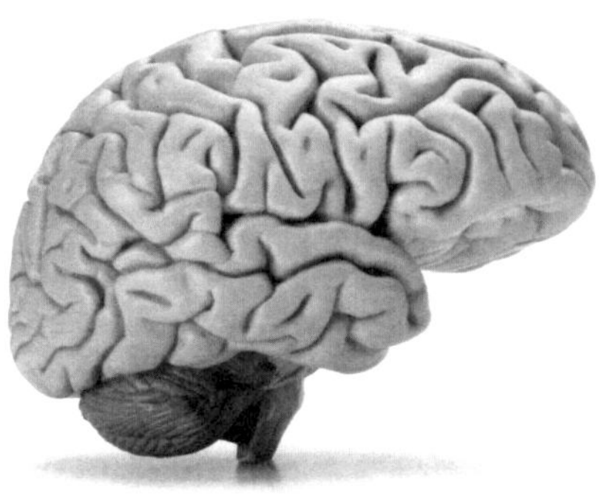

Timeline and Planning for Parent Workshop
(Grades 9-12)

To Get Parents There:

_____ Put date on calendar for Growth Mindset Night

_____ Decide if you are targeting a certain parent group (i.e: students at-risk for failing more than one class, college-bound kids who need help to better manage stress, etc.)

_____ One to three weeks prior to date, send home Parent Flyer (page 72)

_____ Have your administrator do a "shout out" on an email blast or newsletter about upcoming family night, one week prior to the event

To Prepare for the Workshop:

_____ Decide which parent handout you want to use for your program (page 73 or 74)

_____ Consider using Research Review from Chapter 1 for additional handout (page 17)

_____ Make copies of parent survey (page 78)

If using PPT presentation:

____ Download PPT

____ Follow guide on pages 76 and 77

Download the PowerPoint file to guide you through this lesson at: **https://ncyi.org/integratingmindset**

GUIDE FOR PPT for Parent Workshop
(Grades 9-12)

Materials: PPT *from digital landing page above*

Duration: This PPT can last approximately 30 minutes

Preparation: Download PPT from website

Slide # **What to do/say on that slide**

1. (Slide to have up when people enter).
2. Welcome to Growth Mindset night. Ask what grades everyone's children are in, "Raise your hand if you have a 9th grader? If you have a 10th grader?" Etc.
3. Explain the difference between growth mindset and fixed mindset.
4. Share about the vast research showing that when growth mindset is taught, positive outcomes occur in academic and social/emotional responses.
5. Watch the video explaining growth mindset research (from trainugly.com).
6. Reiterate the difference between fixed mindset and growth mindset.
7. Invite parents to think about which mindset they would rather their child have?
8. Look at this image that shows the difference in activity of fixed mindset vs. growth mindset brains.
9. Give an overview of the growth mindset terms being taught to our students (each image is hyperlinked to a video of that concept, so depending on how long you want to make the workshop you could show one of them or all three videos).
10. Explain that one thing taught in the curriculum is a basic understanding of brain science. Review the "hand model" of the brain. Note: If you as presenter want an overview to brush up on this, watch Lori Cross's YouTube on the brain model https://www.youtube.com/watch?v=UNqTviVilH0.
11. Expand on the brain science by describing the concept of "flipping your lid." Note: Read more about this explanation by reading article...*How to Teach Kids About the Brain: Laying Strong Foundations for Emotional Intelligence* at heysigmund.com.

12. Read quote by Daniel Coyle about learning about the brain.
13. Describe the learning process using the example of a baby learning how to run. When you don't know something you are in the "Not Yet" of learning.
14. Play game as described on page 152 "I'm Going to the Moon" to highlight this concept.
16. Share that "The Stairway of Learning" is a good way to think about our attitude about learning. Ask participants to think about which stair they were on for the game we just played. This stairway is good to use with kids when they need to assess their level of motivation.
17. Review the concept of Grit and give reference to Angela Duckworth, PhD. This characteristic has been found to be a common trait among the most successful people in a number of different domains such as: athletics, executive leadership, the armed forces, etc. Note: for review, refer to YouTube core message of the book at: https://www.youtube.com/watch?v=sWctLEdIgi4.
18. Look at this piece of research. The fact that so much research supports the benefits of growth mindset leads us to ask "Why wouldn't we teach about growth mindset to parents? And teachers? And students?"
19. Watch video of the research that has supported the praise of effort vs. the praise of intelligence (on YouTube at https://www.youtube.com/watch?v=NWv1VdDeoRY).
20. Review three ways parents can reinforce growth mindset.
21. Ask attendees to share with a neighbor something they learned in this session.
22. Distribute Parent Quiz and Parent Handout (page 73 and 74). Allow parents to take the quiz, then review the answers.
23. Any questions? Thank them for attending and hang around for questions.

Option: Do a raffle for door prizes.

Parent Growth Mindset Workshop Survey

Excellent = 4 Good = 3 Fair = 2 Not Yet = 1

1. Presentation:

4 3 2 1

2. Video Clips:

4 3 2 1

3. Handout(s):

4 3 2 1

4. Overall:

4 3 2 1

5. What were the most helpful aspects of the program?

____

____

____

6. What can be improved?

____

____

____

9. Are there other workshops that you would be interested in attending? If so, what topics would be of interest to you?

____

____

____

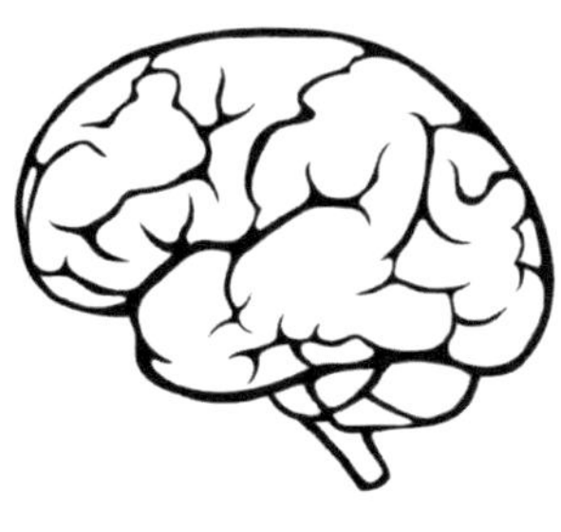

CHAPTER FOUR

4

Growth Mindset Infused in School-Wide Programs

SECTION ONE

Testing, Growth Mindset, and Grit

This chapter will outline ways to integrate growth mindset ideas into programs that are already in place at your school. Use the framework of systems already in place, and add a growth mindset twist using ideas here. Include the following:

• Connecting Growth Mindset, Testing, and Practical Ideas

• Staff Handout

• Handout for Parents on Testing, Growth Mindset, and Grit (Elementary Grades)

• Email for Staff for Statewide Testing Week

• Interactive Lessons: Test Prep Centers for Students, Etc.

• GRIT Word Search

Connecting Growth Mindset and Testing

A concept often talked about in conjunction with growth mindset is grit. Angela Duckworth, PhD, the psychologist credited with pioneering the research on grit, says "One thing we've found, is that children who have more of a growth mindset tend to be grittier."*

So, what is grit? Grit is defined as passion and perseverance to achieve goals. Part of having grit is the ability to stick with things, even in the midst of adversity, in order to accomplish the goal. Being gritty, as it is sometimes called, is a skill needed in test-taking. And with the pressure often put on teachers and students, talking about grit as a school-wide initiative is a great way to encourage students to have a strategy for dealing with the stress testing can stir up. I often tell students that testing is just as much about testing their grit as it is about testing their knowledge of content. I discuss the skill of being able to move forward through "analysis paralysis," or a total melt-down, when a question is too hard or seems too confusing. The ability to stay focused on completing the task is a valuable part of grit needed during testing time.

Duckworth says that non-cognitive skills such as grit and perseverance are just as important as cognitive skills, as it relates to testing. ** Focusing on non-cognitive skills gives students empowerment to have control over knowing how to show effort on a test, even if they don't know the answer to a particular question.

What are Practical Applications in School ?

- As a staff, you can send home information about grit and testing (see page 85)
- Administrators/Counselors can send emails to staff about grit and testing (see page 86)
- Grit Awards can be given out in classes (see page 89)
- Test Prep lessons can be centered around grit and having a growth mindset (see page 119 for ideas for center-based lessons)

* ASCD, Educational Leadership, Volume 71, September 2013, pages 14-20

** (Perkins-Gough, D. (2013). The significance of grit. Educational Leadership, 71(1), 14-20.)

Testing and Growth Mindset

What is the connection between Testing and Growth Mindset?

Statewide testing, end of course testing, bubble-in-answers, constructed responses, essay questions, norm-referenced, standards-based…blech. Whatever kind of test it is, the general consensus is that nobody loves them. But **having a growth mindset** can ease the pain of the inevitable realities of testing.

Connecting the concept of grit with testing is a kid-friendly approach parents can stand behind.

First, let's get clarity on what grit is? Grit is the ability to stick with a task and persevere, even when things get tough. Angela Duckworth, PhD, a professor from University of Pennsylvania, is the pioneer of research on grit. The body of research connecting grit and success is worth investigating. To learn about her book in a brief synopsis, watch this video: https://www.youtube.com/watch?v=sWctLEdIgi4.

How can we help students learn testing is a great opportunity to show off the character trait of grit? In the curriculum *Mindset Matters* there is an acrostic (see right) that teaches the major components of adopting a Growth Mindset. In the acrostic, **D** represents **D**etermination and Grit. As we encourage students to proceed in all areas with determination and grit, they will persevere through testing; thereby easing stress and leading to higher performance. In classes where the *Mindset Matters* curriculum has been taught, teachers have noticed students seem to randomly guess less often, and have an increased stamina in completing challenging tasks.

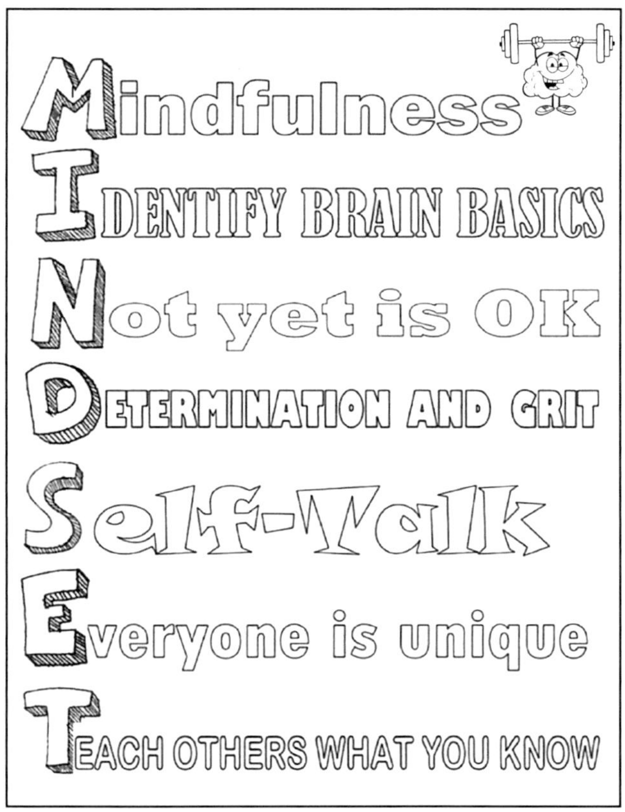

While testing can, at times, be stressful, research has found that students who show **grit and determination** have the best outcomes! Your child has been learning about grit and we wanted to share a little of what we have discussed so you can reinforce these important facts at home.

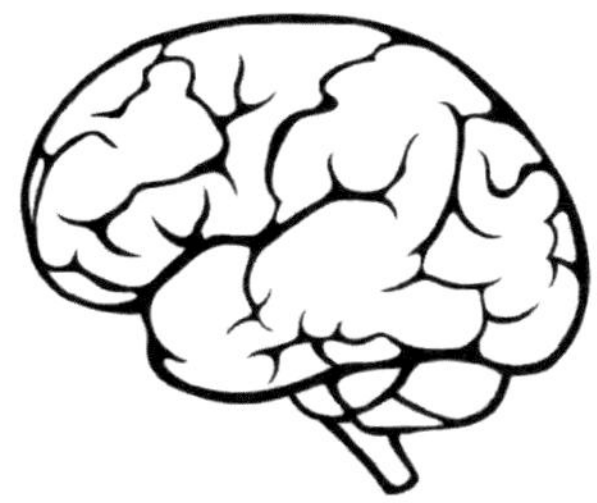

Testing with GRIT

Parents, read this with your child.

What is GRIT?

- **G**ive it your best!
- **R**edo when needed
- **I**gnore giving up
- **T**ake your time

Words that mean the same as GRIT:

- Determination
- Perseverance
- Stamina
- Hard Work
- Not Giving Up

Getting plenty of rest and eating a good breakfast helps a brain function better. Help your kid's brain out. Put them to bed on time, or early, and make sure they have breakfast!

Remind your student that the best way to succeed on tests is to show a quality called GRIT.

Sample Email to Staff the Week before Statewide Testing

Subject: Testing, Growth Mindset and GRIT

Give it your best
Redo when needed
Ignore giving up
Take your time

Teachers,

Testing is upon us and we all have mixed feelings about it: excited, nervous, overwhelmed, or cool and calm. With all our testing feelings comes the attempt to alleviate the stress our students might feel so that they can do as well as possible, without causing undue attention to this process.

HERE IS AN IDEA:

Let's emphasize the importance of GRIT.

- Let's have a **common language** about testing. Let's talk to the kids about GRIT when they are asking questions and expressing themselves.
- You can have a **GRIT Award** each day of testing for students who display that "hard-working don't-give-up" attitude.
- A **parent handout** will be going home that reflects this same language so they can reinforce at home.
- A **video clip** will be available to show your students (with our counselors and admin pumping them up to show "gritty" behavior, which is part of having a growth mindset).

Thanks for all you do in being fantastic and gritty teachers!!

Lisa King, Ed.S, LPC
School Counselor
Blackwell Elementary

I sent this email and received responses like this:

As a parent, I love this!! Granted my kiddos are still in K and 1 and not testing yet, but I can totally see this helping them! Thanks for all that you do and coming up with some awesome tips and strategies to help our students. ☺
– Mandy Spence, PE Teacher

I honestly think it had a HUGE impact on my students. We talked about GRIT A LOT!!!!! For the first time in a number of years I saw students really working and attempting every answer. Not one time did I see anyone "Christmas tree" any section. I was very pleasantly surprised and shocked! My fingers are crossed for good results on the Milestones and the upcoming RI and MI.

Thank YOU for bringing Growth Mindset and GRIT to Blackwell! ☺

– Shirley Crosby, 3rd grade Teacher

Game Show Test Prep Questions

What is one way to show GRIT on the test? *GRIT means "not giving up!"

Imagine you are taking a test and you come to a problem you don't know the answer to. What should you do?

Why is getting a good night's sleep important during testing week?

Why should you eat a healthy breakfast before a big day of learning or testing?

What is a reasonable time to go to bed the night before testing? Can you remind your adults you need to go to bed at this time?

Why do people get nervous about testing? What is one thing you can do to calm yourself down if you get nervous?

What should you do on the test if you finish early?

What will you be thinking if you look around during testing and everyone else seems like they are finished, but you are not?

TEACHER QUESTION:
Teacher please answer this question:
"How do you feel about testing?"

Lack of sleep can:

a. Give you pimples
b. Make you more forgetful
c. Make you want to lose your temper
d. Make it easier for you to get sick
e. All of the above

Name____

GRIT

What You Need To Succeed!

P	D	R	C	L	O	H	G	S	P	C	D	P	S	T
E	S	E	C	O	S	G	E	R	W	Y	A	E	T	P
J	G	V	N	I	N	K	A	S	I	P	E	R	A	M
J	A	A	N	I	A	T	D	O	E	T	R	S	M	E
J	O	I	R	T	M	L	I	R	G	E	F	E	I	T
N	F	E	S	U	E	R	S	N	D	O	O	V	N	T
K	F	I	V	A	O	I	E	I	U	Q	O	E	A	A
E	M	Y	R	T	S	C	T	T	Z	E	R	R	N	G
E	M	N	I	T	B	F	G	O	E	H	P	A	K	O
P	E	G	E	F	O	C	U	S	O	D	R	N	R	F
D	W	N	C	G	B	U	H	J	F	J	W	C	S	Z
U	C	L	U	F	E	S	O	P	R	U	P	E	N	F
E	H	T	A	E	R	B	P	R	A	C	T	I	C	E
G	W	X	S	A	X	A	B	J	Y	S	H	R	F	T
F	C	M	O	E	H	F	W	Z	F	R	Z	H	N	G

Attempt
Breathe
Continue
Courage
Determined
Edit
Finish
Focus
GRIT
Keep
Learned
Mistakes
Perserverance
Persistence
Practice
Purposeful
Proofread
Stamina
Try

How many words did you find?______________

What traits did you need to show to accomplish this? ________________________

____

Give it your best!
Redo when needed
Ignore giving up
Take your time

Give it your best!
Redo when needed
Ignore giving up
Take your time

Example of a GRIT Award.

This can stand alone or be attached to a single serving pouch of…grits. ☺

Give it your best!
Redo when needed
Ignore giving up
Take your time

Give it your best!
Redo when needed
Ignore giving up
Take your time

Connecting College Readiness & Growth Mindset

One crucial component of operating with a growth mindset is to understand that intelligence can grow over time, and skills can be mastered with effort and hard work. This is an important concept for students who are preparing for their future, especially if they are not hearing a "You can be anything you want if you try hard enough," message at home.

As early as elementary school, college readiness skills should be introduced so that students can digest the idea that they CAN seek post-secondary training, even if they have the fears of a) not being able to afford college or b) not having the "smarts" to go to college.

Some of the characteristics needed for success after high school and how they relate to growth mindset are listed below. Furthermore, activities to promote this connection are included in the following pages.

Characteristics of Growth Mindset that Enhance College Success

- Flexibility
- Ability to Deal with Adversity
- Seeking Challenges to Advance Learning
- Understanding Diversity as a Strength
- Innovative Thinking

Cook, Sara L and Komissarov, Sloan and Murray, Brenda L and Murray, James, Predictors for Growth Mindset and Sense of Belonging in College Students (May 31, 2017).

How to Create a College Day at Your School
(Grades K-8)

Many elementary and middle schools have a Career Day. Why not have a College Day, too? You can also combine both and focus on College and Career Week.

> ***"Students who prepare for the future do better in the present."***

You can start small and do one or more of the following to implement a College Day at your school:

- Create a display showing where your staff went to college.
- Have a staff tailgate during a meeting, with pot luck snacks or college themed munchies, (but, darn it, appropriate beverages only!).
- Have teachers show the movie, *Monsters University*.
- Grade levels can compete in a door decorating contest.
- Ask a college student to Skype in and talk about what it's like at school for them.
- College trivia can be shared on the school-wide announcements.
- Invite parents, college-aged siblings, aunts, uncles, etc. to come in and have lunch with their students, wearing college attire.
- Create worksheets with college-related word searches, puzzles and handouts for teachers to use as morning work, if desired.
- Check out the resource *How to Create a College Day* by Lisa King (available on amazon.com).
- Google motivational videos by Inky Johnson to show kids how motivation can help them rise out of the cycle of poverty. https://www.youtube.com/watch?v=NyY9D4nflSw
- Show video *People Like Me Can Go to College* http://bit.ly/2wFmyeJ
- See blog post: http://lisakingcounselor.com/index.php/college-readiness-resources/

Staff can wear shirts representing their alma mater.

Former students can come back and talk about their college experience.

This year, I am graduating from ______________________________.

One day, I'll be graduating from ______________________________.

One day, I'll be graduating from ______________________________.

This year, I am graduating from ______________________________.

"It matters not what someone is born, but what they grow to be."
– J.K. Rowling

Famous Failures Crossword Puzzle

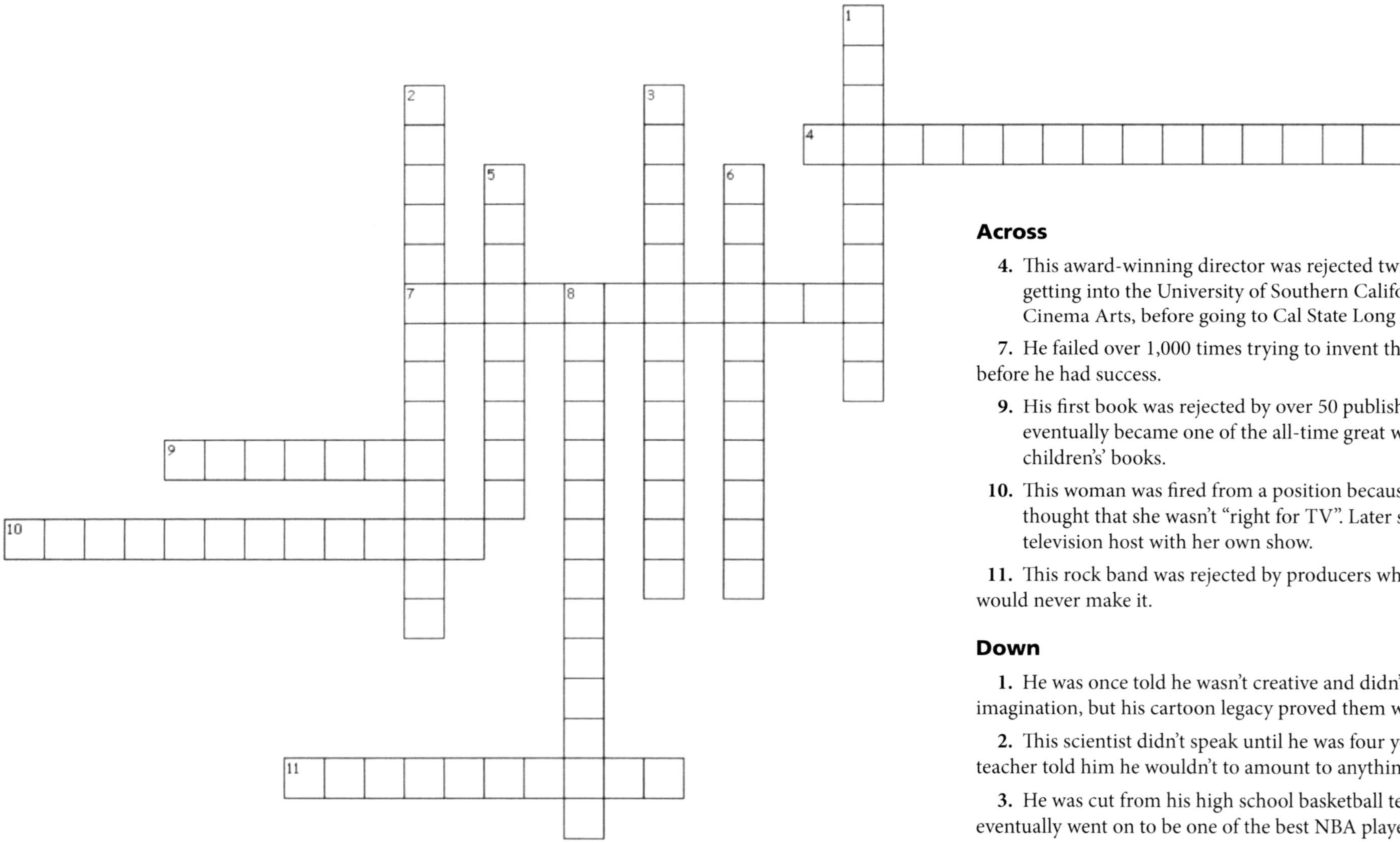

Across

4. This award-winning director was rejected twice from getting into the University of Southern California, School of Cinema Arts, before going to Cal State Long Beach, instead.

7. He failed over 1,000 times trying to invent the lightbulb before he had success.

9. His first book was rejected by over 50 publishers, but he eventually became one of the all-time great writers of children's' books.

10. This woman was fired from a position because her bosses thought that she wasn't "right for TV". Later she became a television host with her own show.

11. This rock band was rejected by producers who thought they would never make it.

Down

1. He was once told he wasn't creative and didn't have any imagination, but his cartoon legacy proved them wrong.

2. This scientist didn't speak until he was four years old. A teacher told him he wouldn't to amount to anything.

3. He was cut from his high school basketball team but eventually went on to be one of the best NBA players ever.'

5. This writer handed in a manuscript titled Harry Potter that was rejected by 12 different publishers.

6. This famous comedian and actress was discouraged by her teachers at a private school of Theater and Dance, who told her mother she was "wasting her money on the school for this girl with no talent."

8. This politician was defeated in 8 elections before becoming one of the most famous presidents in history.

Word Bank:

Abraham Lincoln	J.K. Rowling	Albert Einstein
Michael Jordan	Oprah Winfrey	Walt Disney
Dr. Seuss	Thomas Edison	Lucille Ball
	Steven Spielberg	The Beatles

Growth Mindset Impacts College/Career Readiness

How can we help our students understand that growing intelligence takes time and effort? How can we encourage growth mindset as a college readiness skill?

Read below to better understand the concrete research that shows why operating with a growth mindset is crucial.

FACT: Hochandel and Finamore (2015) found "in an academic environment that teaches grit and fosters growth, students can learn to persist."

FACT: Cook et al (2017) measured more than 2,000 students' mindset across several universities. They found evidence that instructor feedback on student writing had a positive effect on students' mindset and level of perseverance. https://papers.ssrn.com/sol3/papers.cfm?abstract_id=2981141

FACT: In an article by Yeager et al (2016), it was stated that "teaching a lay theory before college narrows achievement gaps at scale." Positive outcomes included "increased full-time enrollment rates, improved grade point averages, and reduced overrepresentation of socially disadvantaged students among the bottom 20% of class rank." http://www.pnas.org/content/113/24/E3341.short

Implication for Educators: Educators can teach the theory of growth mindset which reinforces understanding how to deal with mistakes, the power of yet, and the need for grit. Paunesku's research showed that a brief intervention of teaching growth mindset in high school raised students' grade point averages in their classes, so as educators let's:

- Model Growth Mindset
- Teach GRIT
- Give Constructive Feedback

Connecting Peer Mentoring Programs with Growth Mindset

Having a role model is important for students so they have someone to emulate. This quote seems relevant for the peer helping and mentoring programs:

> ***"Give students someone to imitate."***

Peer mentoring programs have been shown to be effective by enhancing students' sense of connectedness (Angus and Hughes, *Education Leadership Review of Doctoral Research*, v4 p69-84 Spr 2017). As noted throughout this book, growth mindset attitudes also positively affect student change. Why not combine the two?

What mentoring practices does your school already have in place? Think about infusing the mentoring program with growth mindset concepts. The email below can be sent to teachers to build a list of students who would benefit from being mentored.

Sample Email to Staff about Peer Mentors

Teachers,

Would you like a mentor for your class, first thing in the morning, to help one or two of your students? If you have students who could use someone to help them with morning work or work in the hall with them on reading, math, test review, or finishing up homework, please let me know.

In the coming weeks, I will be meeting with Peer Mentors who will be trained to help your students, both with academic work and a sense of school connectedness. Research shows that this connection with older students really works, and this year we are adding a growth mindset component when training the mentors. The Mindset Mentors will be helping students who might be struggling with confidence or need a caring older student to be a role model.

I will open this up to other teachers later this week, so let me know if you are interested. My hope is that this program will be beneficial to mentors and mentees, alike.

Thanks,

Lisa King
School Counselor

Mindset Mentors Overview

This program can be adapted to any age group where there are older students working with younger students. The older students serve as mentors, reinforcing the concepts of growth mindset in weekly interactions.

- Identify student leaders in an upper grade who want to be mentors to younger students.
- This group (whether it be gifted students, peer helpers, or a group of at-risk students) will be trained with PPT materials (see page 136) on the concepts of growth mindset.
- Use a Needs Assessment (sample on page 167) to select a group of younger students who could use an encouraging mentor.
- Set up a schedule that allows the mentors to check in on their mentees at least once a week.
- Meet with Mindset Mentors periodically to answer questions and ask for the students' feedback about what they are doing to successfully help teach growth mindset to other students. Remind Mentors to avoid trying to "convince" mentees of the value of growth mindset, but instead model growth mindset behavior, and frame it as facts about the brain.

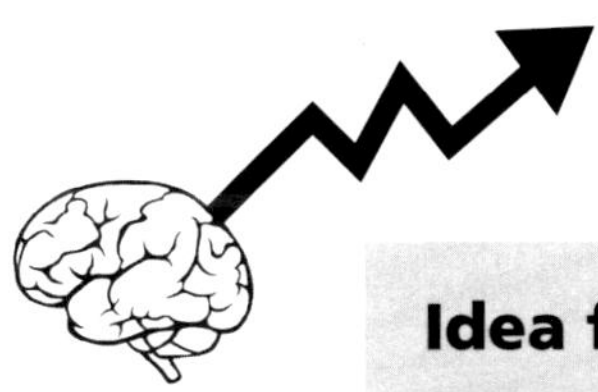

Idea for Documentation of Outcomes and Data:

Collect data on pre/post academic achievement (outcome data) and pre/post surveys (perception data). See Data Chapter for details. For example, you can document reading Lexile scores through the year for the mentees and mentors to see if this experience impacted academic achievement and/or their self-perception.

Mindset Mentors Training Session

Once you have chosen your Mindset Mentors students, invite them to a training session. Below is a sample format of a training session.

Procedures:

1. Have all mentors introduce themselves. Let them know they will be learning about growth mindset so they can work with mentees in modeling and communicating the language of growth mindset and the power of yet.

2. Hand out pre/post survey on page 167.

3. Ask mentors, "what advice would you give to a younger student who might say things like?":

   - "I'm just no good at math." (You could suggest encouraging the student to say, "I am still working on getting better at math).
   - "I could never become a good athlete." (You could suggest encouraging the student to say, "I haven't mastered that sport YET").
   - "I'm just an angry person, and I'm not going to change…" (You could suggest encouraging the student to say, "I need to find some new ways to handle my anger.)

4. Review the concepts of growth mindset by following the lesson plan on page 136 (with PPT that can be downloaded).

5. Assign Mentors the classes they will be going to, or the specific students they will be helping.

6. Review expectations of respect and leadership skills when working with their mentees.

7. Tell mentors there will be periodic check-ins as a group, to monitor progress and share best practices.

Integrating
Growth Mindset
in ***Schools***

CHAPTER FIVE

5

Innovative Ideas for Interactive Lessons on Growth Mindset

Introduction

As we've learned, part of having a growth mindset is to strive to get better at something. Therefore, it would follow suit that growth mindset lessons should be innovative. As with most lessons, it is also helpful if they are meaningful and practical, and of course, teaching with structure makes it easier for both educators and students. In Chapter One, you saw how you can teach the concepts of growth mindset by using the acrostic as outlined on page 102. Any age group can use this structure as a springboard to reach a higher understanding of what it means to adopt a growth mindset. While I have designated the lessons here into section one and section two by grade levels, I encourage you to read both sections, as many of the lessons can be adapted up or down. It is likely that ideas within this chapter will spark ongoing innovations for how you can deliver a growth mindset lesson to your class regardless of which section it is in.

In this chapter, I've provided tools that can help as you introduce the concept of growth mindset in K-12 lessons.

Mindset Acrostic Poster: (page 102) This can be used in groups of classes by either handing a copy out to each student to color in as each concept is completed, or as a guide for teaching the concept as a whole.

Mindset Chant: While this chant is primarily used in elementary and middle school, it is a great multisensory way to teach children the concepts of growth mindset in a memorable way (to see hand motions that go with the chant, visit http://lisakingcounselor.com/index.php/2017/03/03/growth-mindset-links-you-said-you-wanted/).

As seen on page 102, the following concepts make up the content of how to teach growth mindset:

- **M**indfulness-providing a basic understanding of being in the here and now. This can help with stress management techniques in learning academics, as well as dealing with adversity.
- **I**dentify Brain Basics-understanding the basic brain functions and the basic tenants of neuroplasticity are integral parts of growth mindset.
- **N**ot Yet is OK-the concept that if you don't understand something, in reality, you don't understand it YET.
- **D**etermination/Grit-passion and perseverance for a long-term goal is the definition of grit. Teaching students about sticking with it for the long and short term are important parts of learning to achieve and grow.
- **S**elf-Talk-reframing negative self-talk and learning to look at things in a growth mindset framework; training the brain to think differently helps us move past obstacles.
- **E**veryone is Unique-accepting that we all learn differently and knowing we can all achieve greatness, but perhaps in different ways and areas of life that we are passionate about.
- **T**each Others What You Know-this concept aligns with being able to teach a concept once you master it. Encouraging students to be ambassadors of growth mindset allows them to digest the information and embrace teaching it to others.

Mindfulness

Identify Brain Basics

Not yet is OK

Determination and Grit

Self-Talk

Everyone is unique

Teach Others What You Know

Notes and Ideas

Use this as a notes page for supplemental ideas you have to infuse into your lessons on these topics.

TOPIC	NOTES
Mindfulness	
Identify Brain Basics	
Not Yet is OK	
Determination and GRIT	
Self-Talk	
Everyone is Unique	
Teach What You Know	

SECTION ONE

Interactive Lessons
Grades K-8

This section provides examples of how to teach growth mindset concepts in grades K-8. There is a PPT for a 15-30 minute one-time lesson (differentiated by grade level) as well as other interactive lessons:

- Introduction to K-8
- For a One-time Lesson
    - PPT for Students Grades K-2 Introduction to Growth Mindset
    - PPT for Students Grades 3-8 Introduction to Growth Mindset
- Innovative and Interactive Ideas to Teach Growth Mindset
    - Growth Mindset Small Group Book Clubs
    - Centers
    - Scoot

Introduction to K-8

Implementing innovative lessons for students in grades K-8 gives you a chance to step out of your comfort zone and try new ideas. That's demonstrating your own growth mindset, right?! Kids in elementary and middle schools love to dive into creativity if given the option.

It is possible to weave a growth mindset theme throughout your office, lessons, and school climate. You can create a Brain Station (see photo below) or bring a Brain Box (see photo right) to your lessons with worksheets or props inside.

Kids are visual learners. They also get excited when there's the sense of surprise. Why not put a clue for each lesson in your brain box? This visually gives students a connection bewteen "learning about brains" and your lessons.

Having a space in your office designated as a "Brain Station" is a great place for students to spend time as a cool down spot or for enrichment and learning.

Download the PowerPoint file to guide you through this lesson at:
https://ncyi.org/integratingmindset

GUIDE FOR PPT for Grades K-2 STUDENTS

Materials: PPT *from digital landing page above*, Growth Mindset story book (choose from a book such as *Bubble Gum Brain* by Juila Cook or the *Fantastic Elastic Brain* by JoAnn Deak)

Duration: This PPT can last from 15-30 minutes

Preparation: Download PPT from digital landing page at ncyi.org (https://ncyi.org/integratingmindset). If you are traveling to classes to do this lesson, ask each teacher to pull up the PPT before your arrival, to save time.

Slide # **What to do/say on that slide**

1. Tell students today they will be learning about growth mindset and the power of yet.
2. Teach students the Mindset Chant. While it's a fun chant to do, it also has words that weave their way through the concept we are learning today.
3. Begin by saying, "A baby isn't born knowing how to run…."
4. Continue, "First a baby crawls, and then walks, and THEN runs. The walking and crawling are the NOT YET. We all have that period of NOT YET in the time before we know how to do something."
5. Tell students, "We will now watch a short 2-minute video to explain more about how the brain grows as we go from NOT YET into knowing how to do things. This happens through the hard work of brain cells called neurons. Let's learn more from this video called Ned the Neuron (hyperlinked in the slide).
6. Say, "Now let's review our Mindset Chant line by line to see how it has to do with this concept of growth mindset… knowing that your brain grows. For example, first you have to know addition before you can learn multiplication. You have to train your brain."
7. Say, "You have to learn the alphabet before you can learn to read." (Why do you need to learn to read? To show the world you know how to do it).
8. Say, "You will get to be really good at some skills if you work on them. For instance, some of you are very good at video games because it is what you work on."
9. Say, "Think about what skill you work on a lot. Whatever you work on is what you will be good at; whether it is sports, or writing, or being kind or learning a musical instrument ."

10. Say, "Now let's think about something you might not know how to do." Ask for volunteers who can share one thing they don't know how to do. When the person says their sentence "I don't know how to __________" the rest of the group will say in unison "YET".

11. If there is time, read a book with a growth mindset/not yet theme. See page 112 for examples of titles that can be read.

12. Ask participants to share with a neighbor what they learned in this lesson. To wrap up this lesson, watch a music video about the power of yet (see the Janelle Monet song hyperlinked in the slide).

"Love the idea that teaching children to recognize they can learn via teaching them about their brain is invaluable!"

– Diane Ryan, School Counselor
Columbia, South Carolina

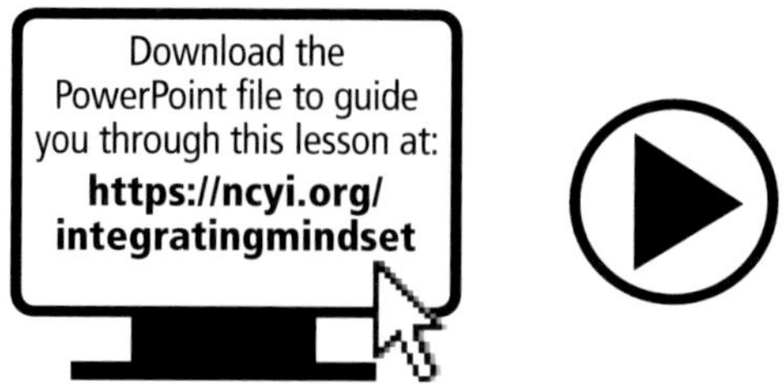

GUIDE FOR PPT for Grades 3-8

Materials: PPT *from digital landing page above.*

Duration: This PPT can last from 15-30 minutes

Preparation: Download PPT from digital landing page at ncyi.org (https://ncyi.org/integratingmindset). If you are traveling to classes to do this lesson, ask each teacher to pull up the PPT before your arrival, to save time.

1. Tell students today they will be learning about growth mindset and the power of yet.
2. Say to students, "Turn to the person next to you and answer this question: "What is Growth Mindset?" If you don't know, you can say "I don't know what growth mindset is yet." Or if you know, but can't explain it say, "I can't explain it yet."
3. Review what growth mindset means.
4. Say "Let's look at this student who is saying some growth mindset phrases."
5. Tell the students why is it important to learn about growth mindset.
6. Review the MINDSET acrostic (page 102), describing the components of growth mindset.
7. Teach students the Mindset Chant.
8. Tell participants about the POWER OF YET. If you can't do something, realize that you just can't do it yet.
9. Say, "Now, let's play a game. This game is called 'I'm Going To he Moon.'" (see directions on page 152)
10. If there is time, you can do this activity. Say "Now, let's play a game called "Whoops Johnny" (see directions on page 151).
11. Ask participants which step they were at on the 'The Stairway of Learning" when they were playing this game. Think about what step you are on when you are doing math, cleaning your room, or learning a new song. If you don't know how to do it, remember that you just don't know how to do it YET. You just have to keep climbing the staircase, ie: putting forth effort.
12. Review the concepts of Fixed vs. Growth Mindset with the video hyperlinked on the PPT slide (duration 3 minutes 30 seconds).

Book Clubs: Bibliotherapy In Action

Teachers and counselors like to read aloud and students enjoy listening to stories read aloud by adults. There are connections students often make to "seeing themselves" in a story and reading aloud offers an engaging and easy-to-plan small group format.

According to Wikipedia, the term "bibliotherapy" was coined in 1916 by Samuel Crothers to refer to the process in which reading a book can be used to change behavior. One way to run a group is to use bibliotherapy and call it a book club. Below are options for running a book club.

Option 1: Chapter Books for Growth Mindset Book Club (See Page 114)

Option 2: Picture Books Book Club (see below)

To have a small group focused on growth mindset, choose books that meet your objectives.

For instance, are you going to focus on understanding that mistakes are an essential part of learning? Then focus on one of these books each time you meet.

Do you want to focus your small group on grit and working hard through adversity? Check out this website for ideas on books you can read in group. There are many other books to add to this small group idea. (https://imaginationsoup.net/2016/05/10/30-biographies-model-growth-mindset/)

Book Clubs can also be run by following the acrostic on pages 112 and 113 and then reading one book from each of the components of MINDSET and discussing them in respect to how growth mindset is shown in each book. Choose one book from each topic below to read with your group.

Condensed Bibliotherapy List Elementary

Mindfulness

What Does It Mean to Be Present? By Rana DiOrio
Mindful Monkey Happy Panda by Lauren Alderfer
Moody Cow Meditates by Keri Lee MacLean
Peaceful Piggy Meditation by Kerry Lee Maclean and Kerry Maclean
Sitting Still Like a Frog by Eline Snel
You are a Lion by Taeeun Yoo
I am Peace: A Book of Mindfulness by Susan Verde and Peter Reynolds
Charlotte and the Quiet Place by Deborah Sosin
Puppy Mind by Andrew Jordan Nance
The Lemonade Hurricane: A Story of Mindfulness and Meditation by Licia Morelli

Identify Brain Basics

Your Fantastic Elastic Brain by Joann Deak
A Walk in the Rain with a Brain by Edward Hallowell and Bill Mayer
Think, Think, Think: Learning About Your Brain by Pamela Hill Nettleton
Young Genius: Brains by Kate Lennard
Bubb1111le Gum Brain by Julia Cook

Not Yet is OK

Everyone Can Learn to Ride a Bicycle by Chris Raschka
Leo the Late Bloomer by Robert Kraus
Thanks for the Feedback (I Think) by Julia Cook
Beautiful Oops by Barney Salzberg
Emily's Art by Peter Catalanotto
Sergio Makes a Splash by Edel Rodriguez
The Thing Lou Couldn't Do by Ashley Spires
The OK Book by Amy Krouse Rosenenthal and Tom Lichtenheld
Rosie Sprout's Time to Shine by Allison Wortche

Determination and Grit

Grit & Bear It! By MS Zentic
Stuck by Oliver Jeffers

Bounce Back! A Book About Resilience by Cheri J. Meiners M.Ed.

Wilma Unlimited by Kathleen Krull

Samantha on a Roll by Linda Ashman

Winners Never Quit by Mia Hamm

Sally Jean Bicycle Queen by Cari Best

The Race by Caroline Repchuk

Self-Talk

Tiger, Tiger Is It True? by Byron Katie and Hans Wilheim

No Biggy by Elycia Rubin

Carla's Sandwich by Debbie Herman

A Happy Hat by Cecil Kim

Don't Feed the Monster on Tuesday by Adolph Moser

It's Tough to Lose Your Balloon by Jarrett J. Krosoczka

Good News, Bad News by Jeff Mack

Some Dogs Do by Jez Alborough

Rain Brings Frogs by MaryAnn Cocca-Leffler

The Worst Day of My Life…EVER! By Julia Cook

One of Those Days by Amy Krouse Rosenthal

Everyone is Unique

Calvin Can't Fly by Jennifer Berne

Only One You by Linda Karanz

You Be You by Linda Krantz

Rosie's Story by Martine Gogoll

The Sneetches by Dr. Seuss

It's OK to be Different by Todd Parr

Hooray for You: A Celebration of You-Ness by Marianne Richmond

Eggbert: The Slightly Cracked Egg by Tom Ross

Back to Front and Upside Down by Claire Alexander

Teach Others What You Know

Although there isn't a book list for this, it's important to allow students to re-teach any of the concepts they have learned to show mastery.

Chapter Books for Growth Mindset Book Club

For older students, chapter books can be read together in a book club setting. These sessions can look different to meet your needs. If you prefer doing a book club "lunch bunch" so less instructional time is impacted, consider scheduling during lunchtime and students can eat while you read the book aloud (or you can listen to an audio book). A few suggestions for Grades 4-8 book club selections are:

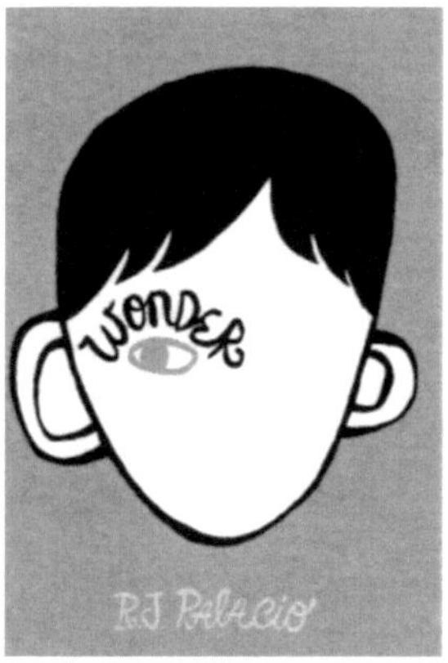

***WONDER* by RJ Palacio**

Idea: Have students create their own *Wonder* Self-Portrait along with a precept that speaks to them.

Here is a photo of the canvases created in a *Wonder* Book Club.

***Hatchett* by Gary Paulsen**

Check out the website regarding this book as a great book club selection (http://bit.ly/2fMLcne).

In this post by Keith Geswein titled "The Perfect Book for Teaching Growth Mindset," you will see an overview of the book and some great discussion questions.

Make copies of this "Book Club Reminder" to send to students

You are invited to The Book Club!

When: ______________________________

Where: ______________________________

A Special Invitation to The Book Club!

Date ______________________________

Dear Parents/Guardians,

Your child has been invited to join a small group Book Club that will meet once a week for thirty minutes and last eight to ten weeks. We will read aloud each week and students will participate in discussions, surveys, art projects, and activities aimed at furthering the development of interpersonal skills, while connecting the book to their own lives and insights.
It is my hope that this experience will support the academic and social/ emotional development of your child. If you have any questions or concerns please feel free to call me at the number below. Thank you for your support and consideration.

Sincerely,

____

Please sign and return to _______________________.

_____ Yes, my child_________________________, has my permission to participate.

_____ I prefer that my child not participate in the group.

____

Parent/Guardian Signature Date

Growth Mindset Scoot

Materials: Scoot Cards (pages 116-117), For each student: 1 Scoot Recording Sheet (page 118) and a pencil.

Time Needed: 30-40 minutes

Procedures:

1. Make copy of Scoot Cards on page 116-117. There are blank cards you can use to make a few of your own questions or tasks, as well.
2. Place one card on each student's desk or other tables around the room. You can set this up in numerical order or out of order, it's up to you. It makes it easy for students to navigate through the cards by putting the cards in order…most students like the challenge of searching for the next number.
3. Give each student a Scoot Recording Sheet (on page 118) and a pencil.
4. Identify the sound/signal you're going to use and let students know when they hear the signal, (whether it is you saying "Scoot" or ringing a bell/chime), it is time to move.
5. Now, instruct each student to go to a place where there is a card on a desk/table. They will write their answer to that task card in the corresponding number on their recording sheet.
6. No more than two students should be at a card at a time.
7. After one to two minutes, you'll say "Scoot" (or use another signal). Students leave that card, take their recording sheet with them, and scoot over to another card and get started on that question/task.
8. When time is called (and most students are complete with their card) call the group together to share answers.

1

Do you think you will go to college when you get older? Write: Yes, No, or Maybe?

2

Do five jumping jacks.

3

What does it mean to have a growth mindset?

4

How much do you think a human brain weighs?

5

When you are feeling stress or anger, what do you do to calm down?

6

Do you know what a neuron is? If so, write an explanation. If not, write "I don't know."

7

What is one skill that you want to learn but don't know YET?

8

What are two things you might want to be when you grow up?

9

Take a deep breath in through your nose like you're smelling a flower.

10

Give the teacher a high five!

11

Fill in the blank: You can train your

______________.

12

Write down the name of a person who works hard.

13

What can you say to yourself if you don't understand something?

14

What happens to your brain when you learn a new skill?

15

When you are scared, what does your brain want to do?

16

What is your reaction when you make a mistake?

17

If given a choice, would you pick an easy or difficult puzzle to solve?

18

Growth Mindset Scoot Score Sheet

Name____

1.	2.	3.	4.
5.	6.	7.	8.
9.	10.	11.	12.
13.	14.	15.	16.
17.	18.		

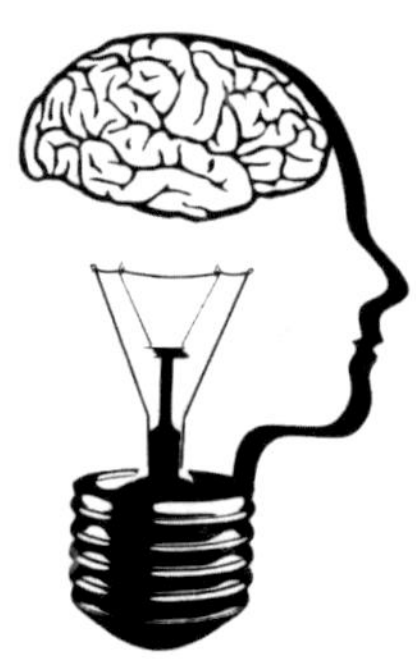

Center Based Learning

To reinforce multisensory learning, you can create centers or stations that provide interactive education.

Overview:

Center-based lessons can be set up in a separate room if you have access to one, or centers can be prepared in mobile portable containers and brought to the classroom in which you are doing the lesson. Each center should be set up in a separate corner or area of the room.

Split students into groups of 5-7 (if your class size is larger, it might be wise to set up multiple centers). Each group will rotate to the different centers set up in various corners/areas of the room. Each center lasts about six minutes, depending on the timeframe of your lesson. Ring a bell at the end of each center time allotment, so students know it is time to rotate.

Sample 30-minute lesson:

- Introduction/Explanation of Centers to Whole Class (four minutes)
- Each of the four centers lasts approximately six minutes (24 minutes, total)
- Conclusion and Wrap Up (two minutes)

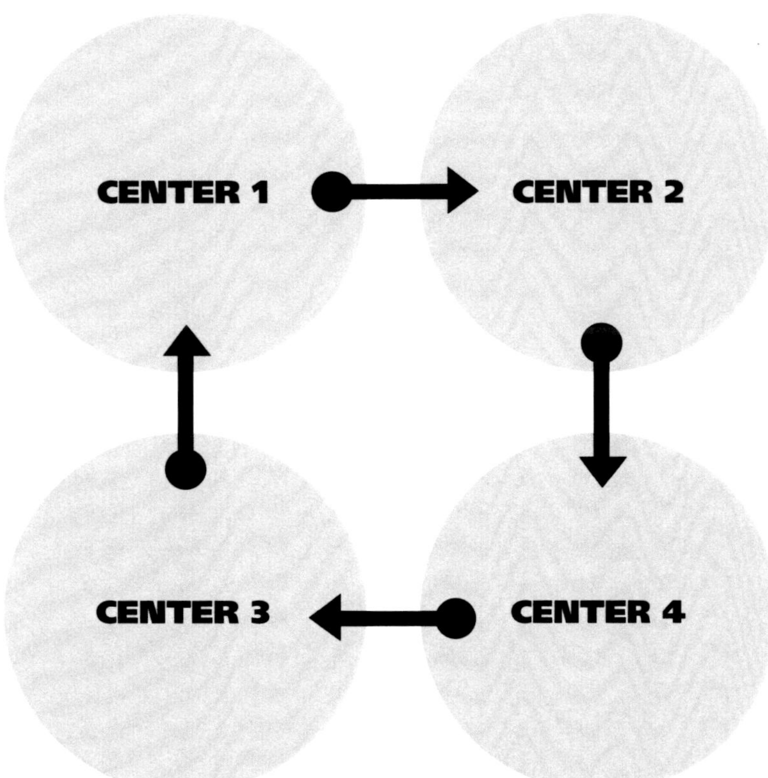

Growth Mindset Centers

Procedures:

1. Decide what activity you want to create for each center.

2. Display descriptive posters in the area along with a Center Number sign (pages 122 and 123).

3. Prior to beginning the center rotations, explain each center to the whole group.

4. Assign students a center number at which to begin. Tell students to listen for the bell or sound that indicates the center is over. Ask students to then straighten up that center and wait for verbal instruction to go to the next center.

There are sample centers below, but any six-minute activity can be used as a center. Other ideas are:

- Create a center to collect data. This can be done on iPad's, computers, or paper. See the Data Chapter for survey ideas.
- See pages 127-132 for options of worksheets to set out for art /activity centers (i.e. Different Types of Smarts, Word Search, etc.).

For a Video Center: here's a list of Growth Mindset Videos that are just the right length for centers (five to six minutes).

Title of Video	Website URL	Duration
SOAR	http://bit.ly/2xxLbfX	6:14
Growth Mindset vs. Fixed Mindset	http://bit.ly/2fJNh38	5:03
9 Proofs You Can Improve Your Brain Power	http://bit.ly/2fgszHw	5:27
Pathway Transformative Initiative -Growth Mindset	http://bit.ly/2jYtlxZ	4:05

Growth Mindset Centers

Center 1: Silent Reading Center

(See page 124) This center can be filled with books about growth mindset and brain science. Have the students write one "fancy fact" they've learned on a sticky note.

Center 2: Puzzle Center

(See page 124) Set up two jigsaw puzzles and tell students they can choose the hard one or the easy one. It's interesting to see who likes to challenge themselves.

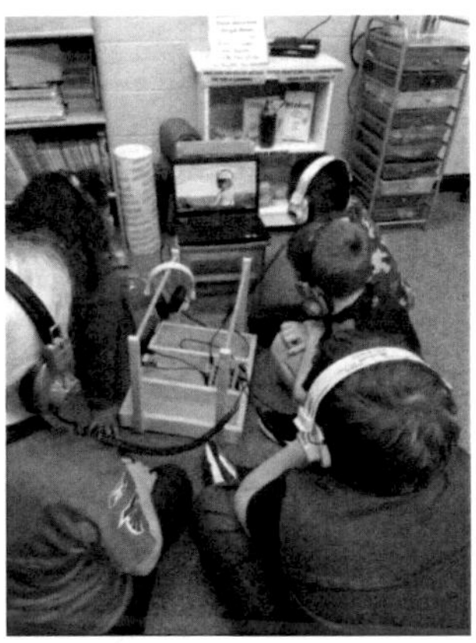

Center 3: Video Center

(See page 125) If you have access to headphones, that can help keep the video center quiet. Showing the video on a laptop or iPad is an engaging way to present growth mindset information.

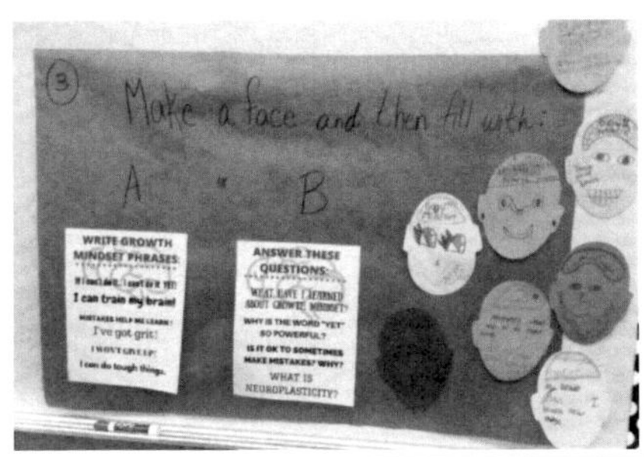

Center 4: Art Center

(See page 126) Have students copy phrases or answer questions on a face they draw or on face-shaped paper (available at Walmart.com – Roylco Face Pad ~$6 for 50 sheets).

Center 1

Center 2

Center 3

Center 4

Growth Mindset

Silent Reading Center

As you read, look for facts about the brain.

Write your favorite fact on a sticky note.

Growth Mindset

Puzzle Center

When something is hard, remember:

YOU'VE GOT GRIT!

Watch this video.

After the video is over, discuss this question with the group: "What did this video teach us about **growth mindset**?"

In your artwork, choose:

A

Growth Mindset

Write Growth Mindset Phrases:

If I can't do it…
I can't do it YET!

I can train my brain!

Mistakes help me learn!

I've got GRIT!

I won't give up!

I can do tough things.

B

Growth Mindset

Answer These Questions:

What have I learned about Growth Mindset?

Why is the word "YET" so powerful?

Is it OK to sometimes make mistakes? Why?

What is "Neuroplasticity?"

Different Types of Smarts

Name____

Fill your brain with different sections of "smart." Label the larger sections for the areas that you feel you are best in. You can create additional sections if you want.

My brain has different types of smarts.

What kind of smarts are there?? The sky is the limit! Some examples are below, but if you have a special talent...then you can fill in that type of smart. Fill in the circle with a color you choose for the type of smart shown, then fill in the brain above. You can also label each part, if you would like.

Math

Reading

Sports

Music

Art

Making Friends

Growth Mindset Word Search

Name____

Directions: Try this worksheet using the word bank below or give yourself a challenge and cover up the word bank to see how many you can find by searching for words that have to do with growth mindset.

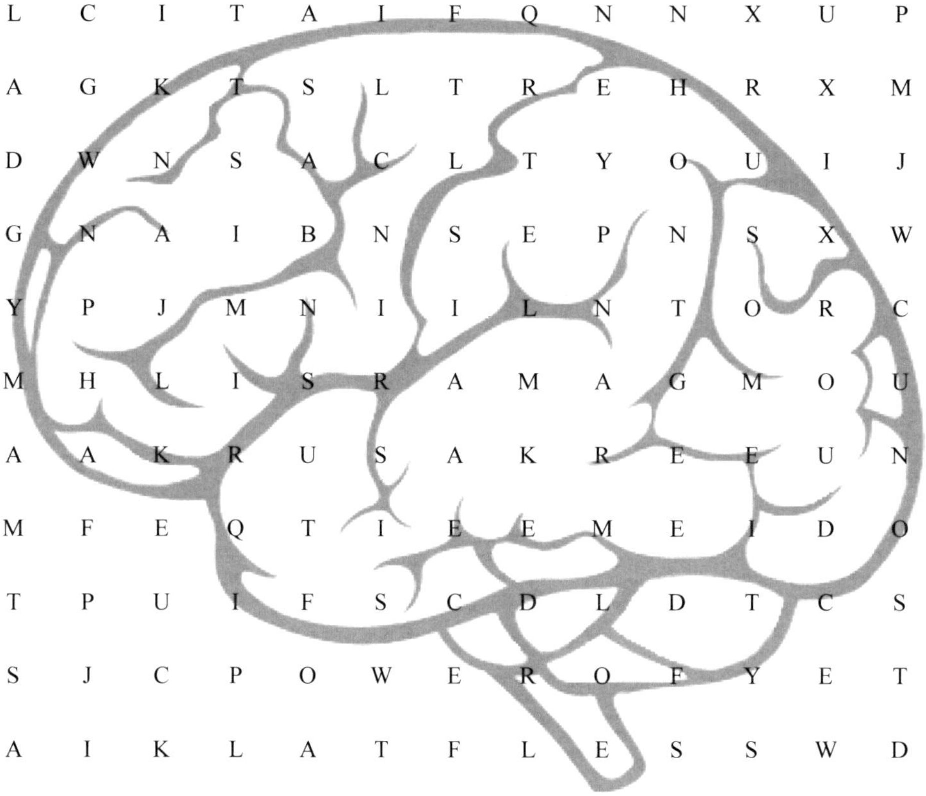

S	N	Y	C	G	X	C	Y	N	C	T	T	E	T	N
S	A	O	X	H	R	A	O	F	S	C	C	M	E	O
E	L	C	I	T	A	I	F	Q	N	N	X	U	P	B
N	A	G	K	T	S	L	T	R	E	H	R	X	M	S
L	D	W	N	S	A	C	L	T	Y	O	U	I	J	T
U	G	N	A	I	B	N	S	E	P	N	S	X	W	A
F	Y	P	J	M	N	I	I	L	N	T	O	R	C	C
D	M	H	L	I	S	R	A	M	A	G	M	O	U	L
N	A	A	K	R	U	S	A	K	R	E	E	U	N	E
I	M	F	E	Q	T	I	E	E	M	E	I	D	O	S
M	T	P	U	I	F	S	C	D	L	D	T	C	S	M
S	S	J	C	P	O	W	E	R	O	F	Y	E	T	G
K	A	I	K	L	A	T	F	L	E	S	S	W	D	W
W	T	R	U	U	A	N	E	U	R	O	N	M	R	M
Y	T	E	S	D	N	I	M	H	T	W	O	R	G	L

AMYGDALA
CHALLENGE
DETERMINATION
GRIT
GROWTH MINDSET
LEARNING
MINDFULNESS
MISTAKES
NEURON
NEUROPLASTICITY
OBSTACLES
PASSION
PERSISTENCE
POWER OF YET
SELF-TALK

Brain Basics Worksheet

Name____

Directions:

1. Label the brain with these two parts: Amygdala, Prefrontal Cortex.

2. Next, fill in the brain using the colors of your choice.

Want a challenge? If so, look up what the other parts of the brain are called and label those parts as well.

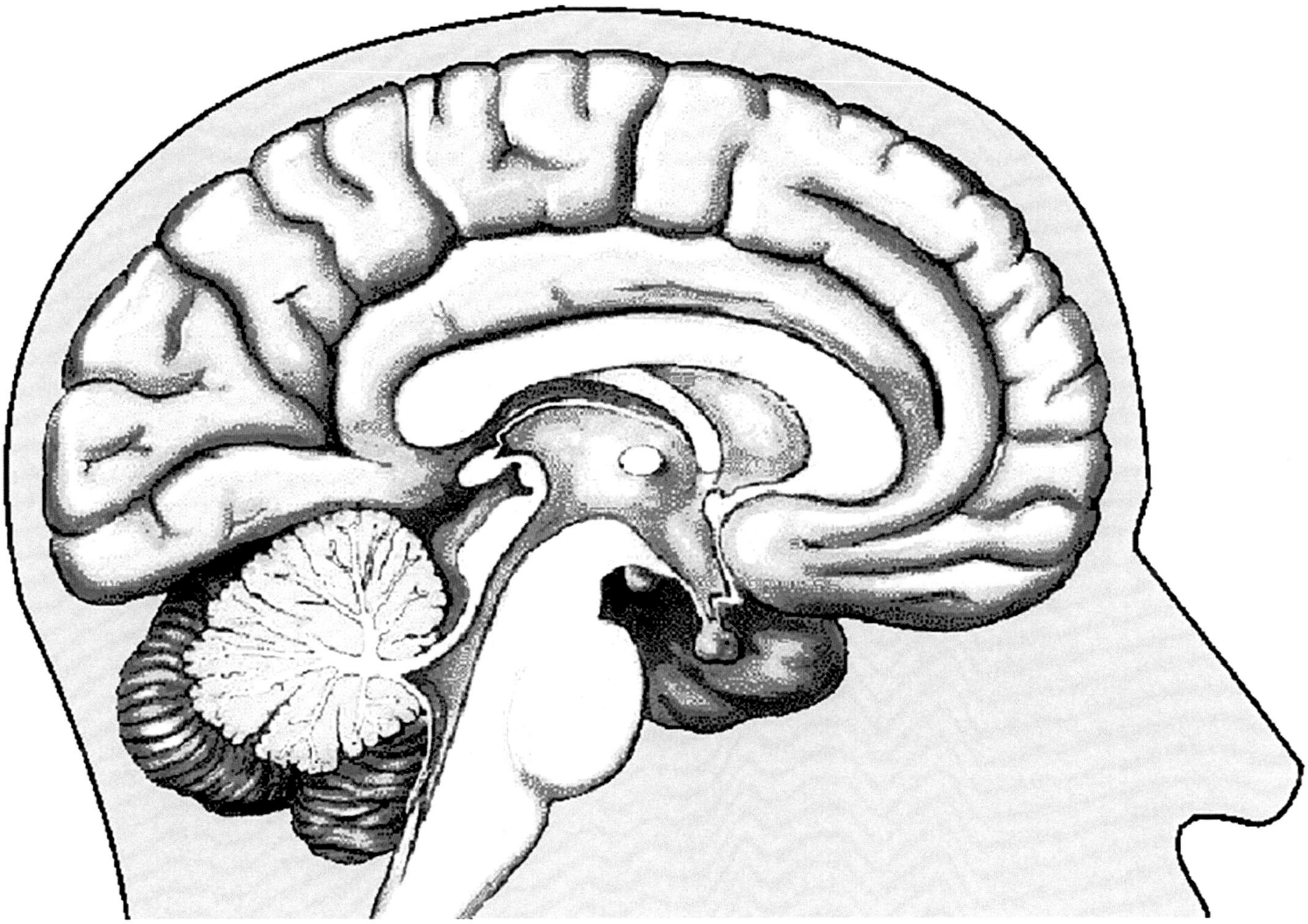

The illustration below (figure A) is a brain cell called a ____ ____ ____ ____ ____ ____.

Uunscramble these letters to find out. **E U N R N O**

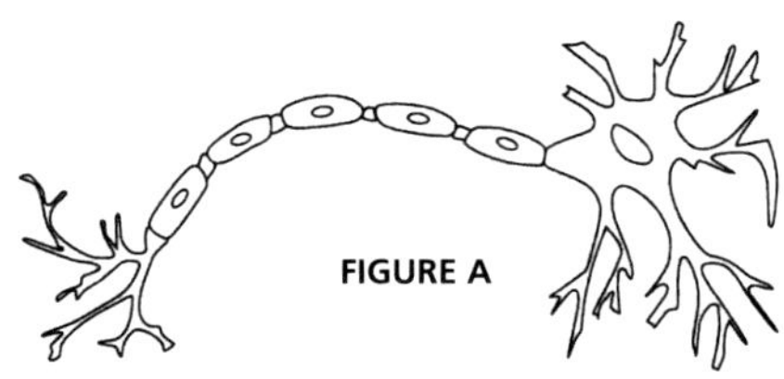

FIGURE A

Brain Model and Flippin' Your Lid

Activity: Can you draw your own brain model on the back of this page? You can draw a hand model or your own version of upstairs brain and downstairs brain.

Look at the hand brain model below.

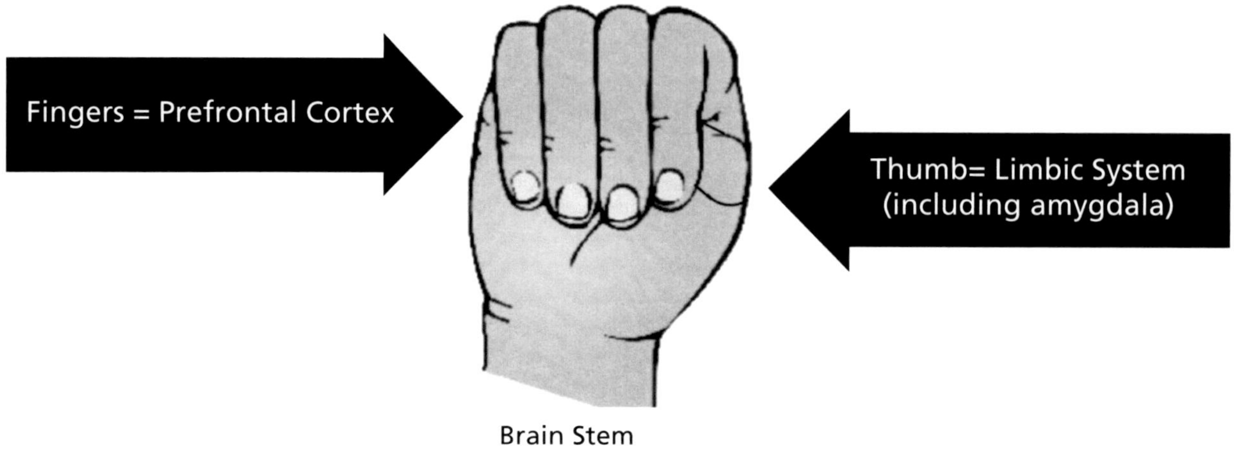

You can also think of the brain in terms of "upstairs brain" and "downstairs brain." Imagine that those who "live" in downstairs brain are the ones who have strong emotions (you can name these characters: Frightened Fran, Angry Adam). Those who live upstairs think clearly and solve problems (Problem Solving Patty, Thinking Theo). If someone in downstairs brain is activated, they cause upstairs brain to flip. When we "flip our lid," we don't think clearly or have good problem solving skills.

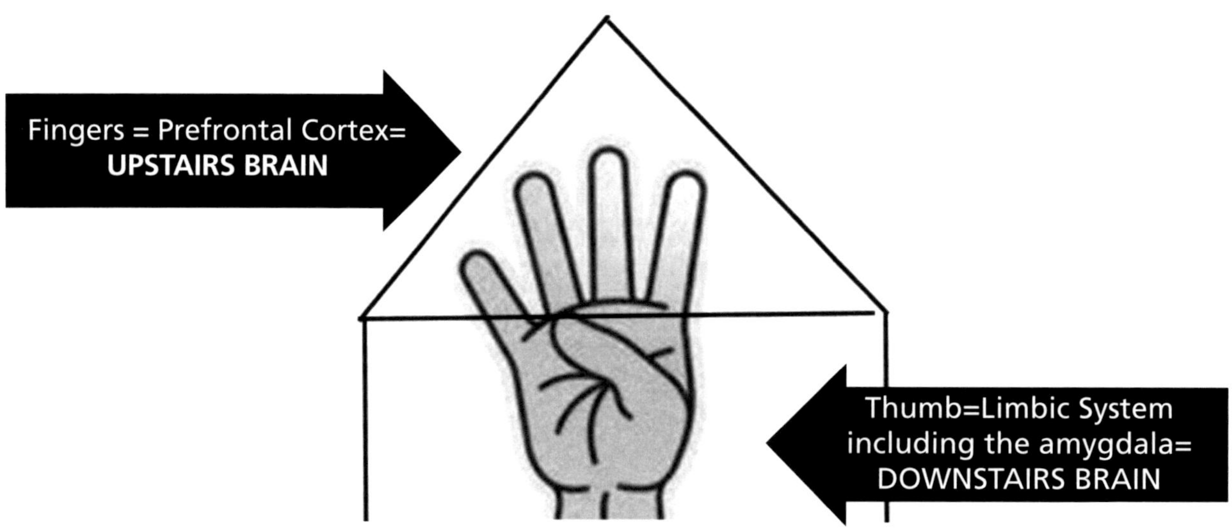

Hand model and flipping your lid analogies adapted from Dr. Dan Siegel lectures as well as the many practitioners who have adopted this way to describe brain basics.

Name____

I can't

____

YET...

But if I train my brain to

____

I will get BETTER and BETTER.

How Many Words Can You Find Within the Phrase…

"GROWTH MINDSET?"

2 Letter Words	**3 Letter Words**
4 Letter Words	**5 (or more) Letter Words**

CHAPTER FIVE

5

SECTION TWO

Interactive Lessons (Grades 9-12)

This section provides examples of how to teach growth mindset concepts in grades 9-12. There is a PPT for a 15-30 minute one-time lesson as well as other interactive lessons:

- For a One-Time Lesson
    - PPT for Students Grades 9-12 Introduction to Growth Mindset
- Innovative and Interactive Ideas to Teach Growth Mindset
    - Growth Mindset Advisement Group
    - Project-Based Learning
    - Mindset Interviews
    - Gamifying: Making Challenges More Fun

Growth Mindset Ideas

Because each school has vast differences, it is difficult to set a prescribed program, small group idea, or lesson that will work in every setting. This chapter is meant to give an outline of several possibilities for your school. Within the following pages lie structured lessons and activities that were created to pave the way to ideas you can implement for your school.

On her website, *The Super Hero Blogspot,* Brittany Wheaton writes that the important tenants of teaching Growth Mindset in Secondary are to:

- Teach your students about the theories, research, and science behind a growth mindset.
- Teach yourself about growth mindset.
- Assign informational text pieces about growth mindset to meet standards.
- Use a growth mindset portfolio to inform, inspire, and educate your students.

http://thesuperheroteacher.blogspot.com/2016/10/teaching-growth-mindset-in-secondary.html?m=1

"I have posters around the classroom with positive ways to use self-talk when difficulties arise while solving math problems. I am also teaching students that all of us can learn math and when we struggle we are growing our brain."

– Tracy Groark, Math Teacher

"To create a growth mindset classroom, my students walk into my room each day and are greeted with a growth mindset question on the white board. All students are encouraged to participate- and they all seem to do a pretty good job of this. I've really enjoyed reading their answers and watching them participate. I've really learned A LOT about the kids that they normally would not share. Along with this idea, we are changing the words in our classroom. We are changing "I can't do this" to always adding "Yet". The power of yet!!"

– Sarrah Davis, Teacher, Triton Jr./High, Bourbon, Indiana

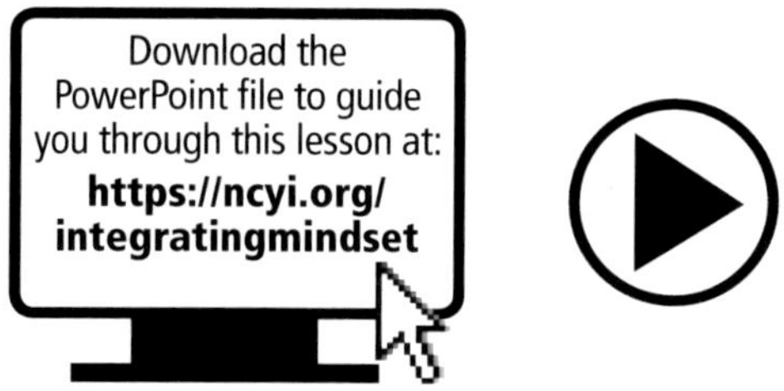

GUIDE FOR PPT for Grades 9-12

Materials: PPT *from digital landing page above.*

Duration: This PPT can last from 30-45 minutes

Preparation: Make copies of Discussion Questions on page 137. Download PPT from digital landing page at ncyi.org (https://ncyi.org/integratingmindset). If you are traveling to classes to do this lesson, ask each teacher to pull up the PPT before your arrival, to save time.

Slide # **What to do/say on that slide**

1. Say, "Today, we are learning about growth mindset."
2. Say, "What is growth mindset?" Click on video to give more detail.
3. Tell the students, "What people have learned is that telling kids to "try" doesn't work. However, showing you how the brain changes when you try, or when mistakes are made… that makes a lot of sense. And there's strong research to support this idea."
4. Show students the research that supports why it is important to learn about growth mindset. Share that kids who learn about growth mindset do better in school and are more equipped to overcome obstacles.
5. Explain the three terms that are important in understanding growth mindset. (Allow kids to choose which video to watch first, as a behavior modification method). All three videos have hyperlinks.
6. Say, "If you want to dive deeper into Growth Mindset… here are other resources you can read and watch."
7. Remind students that you are teaching this because it works.
8. Say, "Although it's not possible, wouldn't it be great if teachers could give you a grade of 'not yet' instead of an F (if they knew you were trying and putting forth effort)?"
9. Invite students to look at the quotes. Ask, "Which quote speaks to you and why? Share with a person near you."

Extension Options:

- Have students answer questions on page 137 and turn in their discussion questions for a raffle. Prizes can be homework pass or other school incentive that your school readily uses.
- Students can create posters with the quotes on page 138, which are also on slide nine.

Name____

Discussion Questions for Lesson: What is Growth Mindset?

Answer the following questions:

1. What is one thing you learned about growth mindset?

2. Why is growth mindset being taught in schools?

3. What do you know about these terms?

GRIT:

NEUROPLASTICITY:

THE POWER OF YET:

Things That Make You Say Hmmm...
Quotes to Discuss

These quotes can be distributed to students for discussion, or used as desk reminders or posters that can be hung in your classroom.

"Your attitude, more than your aptitude, will determine your altitude." – John C. Maxwell	***"The master has failed more times than the beginner has even tried."*** – Stephen McCranie	***"Don't tell me how talented you are. Tell me how hard you work."*** – Arthur Rubenstein
"If parents want to give their children a gift, the best thing they can do is to teach their children to love challenges, be intrigued by mistakes, enjoy effort, and keep on learning." – Carol Dweck	***"Life isn't about finding yourself. Life is about creating yourself."*** – George Bernard Shaw	***"Many of life's failures are people who did not realize how close they were to success when they gave up."*** – Thomas Edison
"If plan A doesn't work, the alphabet has 25 more letters – 204 if you're in Japan." – Claire Cook	***"It's not that I'm so smart, it's just that I stay with problems longer."*** – Albert Einstein	***"Success is the ability to go from one failure to another with no loss of enthusiasm."*** – Winston Churchill

Growth Mindset Advisement

Question: What is Growth Mindset Advisement?

Answer: Growth Mindset Advisement is an eight-week intervention that combines Small Group, Individual Check-Ins, and Goal Setting that leads to positive outcomes for students.

Small Group	*Reinforces* →	**Skill Building**
Individual Check-In	*Reinforces* →	**Accountability**
Goal Setting/Monitoring	*Reinforces* →	**Growth Mindset**

Question: Who should be in this group?

Answer: Use your school's strategic plan to decide which students are performing below expectation. Ask yourself, "In what group is there a need to close the gap?" Look at behavior, attendance, or achievement to select students, along with teacher recommendations. You could also collect perception data (regarding knowledge, attitudes, and skills) using one of the needs assessments on page 167. See Chapter Six regarding more details on collecting data.

Question: What is the structure of this group and how is it different from a typical small group?

Answer: This structure is aimed at combining the benefits of participating in a small group (connecting with peers and creating a sense of belonging) with the benefits of individual advisement (establishing rapport with a caring mentor and having personal accountability for goal setting). The suggested structure is below and samples are on page 140.

- **Session 1:** Group Orientation
- **Session 2:** Group Session
- **Session 3:** Individual Check In
- **Session 4:** Group Session
- **Session 5:** Group Session
- **Session 6:** Individual Check In
- **Session 7:** Group Session
- **Session 8:** Closing Session

Sample Outlines for Growth Mindset Advisement

Sample 1	**Session Ideas**
Session 1: Group Orientation	Review Group Rules, complete pre-survey (page 166) and What is Growth Mindset? PPT(page 136).
Session 2: Group Session	Review main concepts of Growth Mindset mini posters (see Addendum) and introduce PBL Brain Project.
Session 3: Individual Check In	Review with individual students: teacher and/or parent assessment; establish a SMART goal.
Session 4: Group Session	Continue PBL. Do a "Not Yet" game (see page 151-152).
Session 5: Group Session	Discuss Small Bets and Finish up PBL. Watch video "Learning Like a Jungle Tiger" https://www.youtube.com/watch?v=muoVtDjjonM and discuss.
Session 6: Individual Check In	Review SMART goal progress and discuss teacher observations on how student is progressing toward goal.
Session 7: Group Session	Students begin presenting PBL to peers in the group.
Session 8: Closing Session	Students finish presenting PBL to peers in group. Gamifying activity and complete post-survey.

Sample 2	**Session Ideas**
Session 1: Group Orientation	Review Group Rules, complete pre-survey (page 166) and lesson "What is Growth Mindset" PPT (page 136).
Session 2: Group Session	Create Posters with Quotes from "Things that Make You Go Hmm" (page 138).
Session 3: Individual Check In	Review with individual students: teacher and/or parent assessment; establish a SMART goal.
Session 4: Group Session	Do a "Not Yet" game with the group (page 151-152) and discuss The Stairway of Learning See (page 59).
Session 5: Group Session	Discuss and watch video "Learning Like a Jungle Tiger" https://www.youtube.com/watch?v=muoVtDjjonM
Session 6: Individual Check In	Review SMART goal progress and discuss teacher observations on how student is progressing toward goal.
Session 7: Group Session	Do a "Not Yet" game with the group. Have a contest using worksheet "How many Words Can You Find?" on page 132.
Session 8: Closing Session	Complete post-survey.

Sample Email to Staff
Re: Call for Referrals for Advisement Group

Below is an email you can send to teachers to introduce the idea of a Growth Mindset Advisement Group.

Date__________________

Dear Teachers,

With this email, I want to introduce a new program called Growth Mindset Advisement that we will be offering as part of our mission to help students find passion in learning. This program will consist of group and individual sessions with students. Data will be collected to track student improvement with the ultimate goal of student success. Parents and teachers will be made aware of the student's progress throughout the program, and will be asked for feedback on how they perceive goals are being reached.

Topics discussed in Growth Mindset Advisement will consist of:

- dealing with adversity
- basic brain science
- how effort and determination lead to success.

If you have students you would like to refer for this small group experience, please email me your referrals. I'm excited for the opportunity to work with these students!

Sincerely,

Growth Mindset Advisement Permission Slip

Date ______________________________

Dear Parent/Guardian:

Your child has been invited to participate in a Growth Mindset Advisement program. Our primary goal with this program is to ensure your child reaches their full potential. This program will consist of small group sessions to work on school success skills, as well as individual sessions, which will give an opportunity for setting and monitoring personal goals. Your involvement with your child's academics is essential in helping them achieve success. I will be communicating with you through the year about things your child can do to make this a great year.

I look forward to the opportunity to work with your child. Thanks for your support, and please call me if you have any questions!

Sincerely,

____

PLEASE RETURN THIS TO YOUR CHILD'S TEACHER BY ___________________

I give my child, __________________, permission to participate in growth mindset advisement.

I prefer that my child, __________________, not participate in growth mindset.

Parent/Guardian Signature ________________________ Date _____________

Email ____

Growth Mindset Advisement Reminders

Counselor: Use this template to invite specific students to join the Growth Mindset Advisement Group.

You Are Invited!

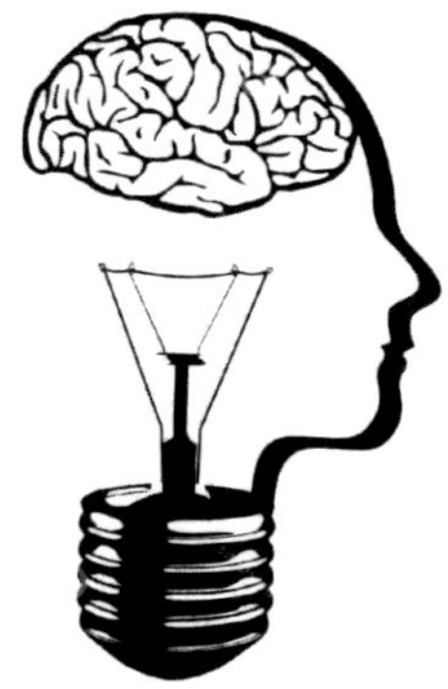

What: **Growth Mindset Advisement**

When: ______________________________

What Time: ______________________________

Where: ______________________________

You Are Invited!

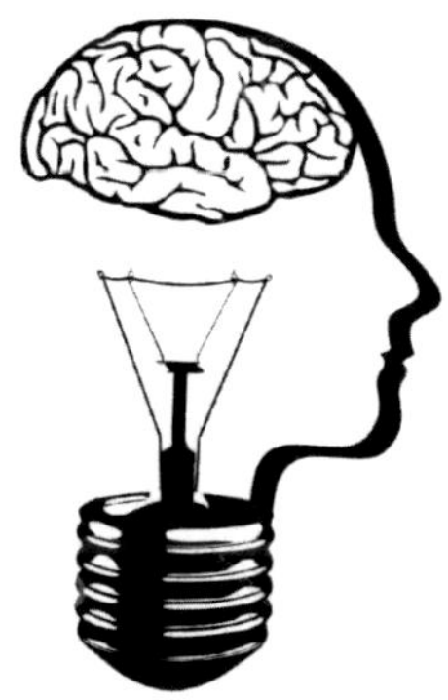

What: **Growth Mindset Advisement**

When: ______________________________

What Time: ______________________________

Where: ______________________________

You Are Invited!

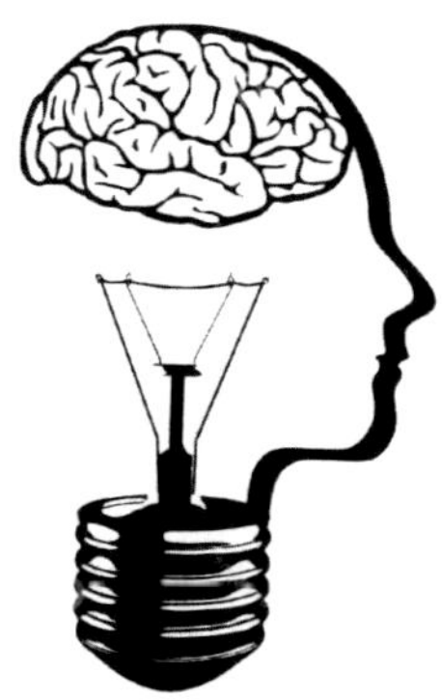

What: **Growth Mindset Advisement**

When: ______________________________

What Time: ______________________________

Where: ______________________________

Project-Based Learning (PBL): Brain Project

> ***"One of the advantages of project-based learning is the flexibility. PBL is an effective instructional strategy within individual content areas, as well as across disciplines. It's engaging for young learners and teens alike."***
>
> – Suzie Boss, edutopia.com July 2014

Project Based Learning (PBL) is a way to allow students to take control of their own learning, by being creative and diving into a world of inquiry, curiosity and self-directed learning. The benefit in having students participate in PBL is "increasing creativity, problem solving, and fluid intelligence, which is the ability to adapt to new experience. This ability to innovate in response to environment, in fact, seems to be the main message of today's brain science," says Thom Markam in his ASCD blog post (read more here: http://edge.ascd.org/blogpost/why-pbl-is-good-for-the-brain).

How do I implement PBL with students?

Tell students they will be given an opportunity to choose a project to work on over the next few lessons. Students will be presenting their finished product to the class.

This product can be anything from a Video, PPT, Song, Presentation, Artwork, Poster, Skit, or Informational Paragraph.

- Instruct students about deadlines for completing the product (some assignments may take 30 minutes, others may need a week; depending on what project is chosen by students to complete.)
- Option for students to present their ideas to the group or for leader to use rubric to give feedback.
- Allow students to work independently or in groups.

Instructor will need to decide how much direction to give to students.

Guided PBL

If the instructor would like to teach a lesson first to give the students some information before setting them free to work on a project, see Options One and Two (pages 145 and 146). Then allow students to reteach part of the lesson in a creative way.

Free Choice PBL

If instructor would prefer to give the students free reign in creating a Brain Project or Growth Mindset Project, students can begin with the planning guide on page 147.

Options for Guided PBL

PBL Option 1: The Brain and Growth Mindset

1. Teach PPT lesson "What is Growth Mindset?" outlined on page 136.
2. Allow students to do self-directed learning by watching all or one of the videos hyperlinked into slide # 6 of the PPT found on page 146 (these videos are also listed below).
3. Students can create a project surrounding the concepts of neuroplasticity, power of yet, grit or any other component that speaks to them on growth mindset.
4. Products can include: Video, PPT, Song, Presentation, Artwork, Poster, Skit, Informational Paragraph, or any other way to deliver information.
5. Students will be given the planning guide (page 147) and the rubric (page 148).

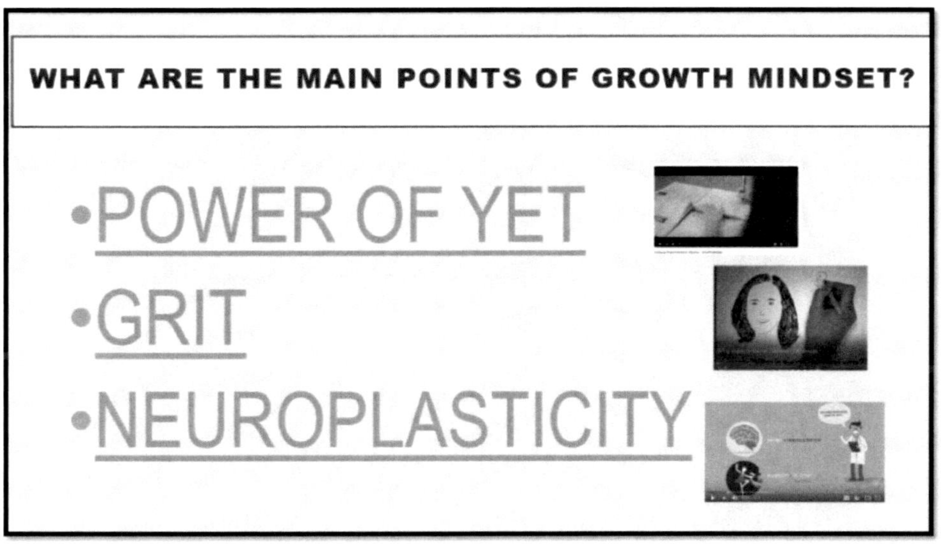

Title of Video	Website URL	Duration
GRIT	http://bit.ly/2xAFAE9	3:50
What is Neuroplasticity?	http://bit.ly/2wVdFBQ	3:14
Pathway Transformative Initiative-Growth Mindset	http://bit.ly/2jYtlxZ	4:05

Continued on next page.

PBL Option 2: Keeping the Brain Healthy

Teach the following mini-lesson before having students choose which concept they would like to expand on.

1. Tell students that the brain uses a huge amount of energy; burning about 30% of the fuel your body uses. We need to take care of our brain so it is functioning at the highest capacity.
2. Tell students "With all the energy your brain uses, you need to be aware of":

   A. **Food:** Your brain needs healthy foods with Omega-3's such as Eggs, Nuts and Fish.

   B. **Sleep:** Think of a phone that needs to recharge. Your brain also needs to recharge for at least 1/3 of each day (8-9 hours of sleep). If not, you forget things more easily.

   C. **Exercise:** Movement and exercise increase breathing and heart rate so more blood flows to the brain. A recent study found that walking actually improves memory.

   D. **Challenges:** Your neural pathways grow and stay defined if they are used. If you challenge yourself, these neurons keep firing and you stay sharper in your skills.
3. After reviewing the above facts, tell students you will now begin Project Based Learning where students will create a product in any way they would like, to teach one or more of the above facts (A, B, C, or D).
4. Products can include: Video, PPT, Song, Presentation, Artwork, Poster, Skit, or Informational Paragraph.
5. Give students the planning guide (page 147) and the rubric (page 148)

Want to learn more about Project Based Learning?

https://medium.com/@spencerideas/collaborative-projects-can-work-in-any-subject-9632f9c2cf00

http://edge.ascd.org/blogpost/why-pbl-is-good-for-the-brain

Project-Based Learning
Brain Project Planning Guide

Name(s) of people working on the project:

____

____

Brainstorm Ideas

What materials will you need?

Title of Project:

____

What are the steps in creating this project?

1.

2.

3.

4.

5.

Project-Based Learning Rubric

Name(s) of people working on the project:

____

____

Title of the Project: ______________________________

	4	3	2	1	Your Score
Use of Time	Used time well. Focused on getting the project done without distracting others.	Mostly focused on getting the project done without distracting others	Used some time well. Some focus on getting project done, but occasionally distracted others.	Did not use class time to focus on the project OR often distracted others.	
Main Idea	The topic and message of the project was presented in an easy to understand format.	Topic and main ideas were presented somewhat clearly.	Topic was given but main ideas were unclear or lacking.	Topic and/or main ideas were absent or very unclear.	
Organization	The design/layout was organized, and visually appealing.	Presentation was attractive in terms of design, organization, and neatness.	Presentation was acceptable, though it could have been better organized.	Presentation was distracting, due to being poorly organized.	
Creativity	There was a great deal of creativity put into the project.	There was some amount of creativity in the project.	There was a minimal amount of creative efforts.	There was no creative effort put forth in this project.	
Total					

Gamifying: Making Challenges More Fun

Question: What is gamifying?

Answer: Gamifying is a term for making something into a game, or a way to make learning fun.

Make achieving a task feel like a game.

Little Bets

Author, Peter Sims, discusses in his book, *Little Bets*, that our fast-paced world is a prime setting for making "little bets" rather than "big bets," since this approach allows you to change your goal as you go along, while learning from the experience of winning or losing little bets.

"Little Bets" is the idea of taking small bets you are willing to lose in order to achieve bigger goals, i.e. "I bet I can finish 10 pages in 15 minutes," or "I bet I can do this math paper in five minutes and then edit it to make sure it's right in four minutes."

Examples:

For class work, have students make little bets on what they can do. Although this sounds like "short-term goal setting," it sounds a lot more fun to "make a bet you can do." If the student wins the bet, give them a good grade for accomplishing the goal.

Peter Sims, author of *Little Bets: How Breakthrough Ideas Emerge from Small Discoveries* tells us:

"What do Apple CEO Steve Jobs, Comedian Chris Rock, and the story developers from Pixar have in common? They all have achieved remarkable results using a surprisingly similar approach of methodically taking small experimental steps."

Want to hear more about Peter Sims book? Listen to a six-minute synopsis on YouTube: https://www.youtube.com/watch?v=TFtAAnSH7FE

Use Games or Challenging Activities to Teach

Games inherently lead to a challenge and the idea of creating an atmosphere of forced struggle lends itself to the concept of "productive failure," a key concept in growth mindset. If we give students the time and space to work through problems, a growth mindset will help them embrace learning through mistakes and struggle. Learning is a process and one that needs to be taught. It's beneficial to use challenging activities and/or games and ask students, "What evidence of growth mindset do you see in playing this game?"

Below are a few fun games that reinforce the concept, "Don't give up even if you don't get it YET." In each of these games, students must use different parts of their "smarts" and different "out of the box" thinking to "get it." If students don't "get the trick," remind them that they just don't get it YET.

If you want to learn more about gamifying and forced struggle, see:

- http://www.theedadvocate.org/how-does-gamification-effect-the-learning-process/

Encouraging Students to Persist through Challenges:

- https://www.youtube.com/watch?v=voa0F2C_hjY

These books are resources full of experiential games that lead to great discussion about learning, life, and the power of yet.

"Not Yet" Games
Promoting Growth Mindset and the Power of Yet

Read these games thoroughly. At first glance, they might seem like they are for a younger crowd, but don't be fooled. These are fun to do with teens and adults to see if they get the tricks.

Games 1-3 have a "trick" that the audience needs to catch to "get it" with virtually no preparation needed. Games 6-8 require some preparation but are great games that teach the power of yet and the importance of persistence.

1. Whoops Johnny:

Hold out your hand, palm facing the audience, with all five fingers spread. Tap the top of each finger with the index finger of the other hand (starting with the pinky) and as you do so say "Johnny." Slide down from the index finger to the thumb while saying, "whoops Johnny, whoops Johnny." Then go back and tap each finger now starting with the pointer and as you do so say "Johnny."

So it sounds like this...

Johnny, Johnny, Johnny, Johnny

Whoops Johnny, Whoops Johnny!

Johnny, Johnny, Johnny, Johnny.

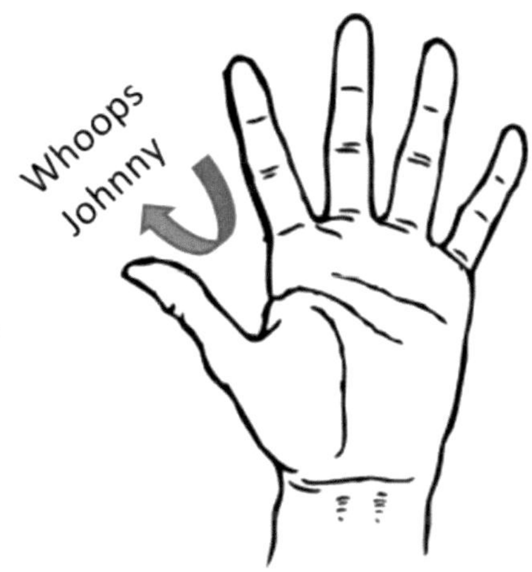

The trick: Fold your hands in front of your body after doing the hand motions. If the participants get that move, regardless of how they do the hand motions, then they get it!

2. I Can Do the Pencil Dance:

All you need is a pencil. You lift it and hold it any which way and do a little dance of any kind. Say or sing "I can do the pencil dance, pencil dance, pencil dance. I can do the pencil dance, how 'bout you?"

The trick: Clear your throat before you start the pencil dance (it doesn't matter how you move the pencil or how you dance or sing the song. The only thing that participants need to do to "get it" is clear their throat).

Continued on next page.

3. I'm Going to the Moon:

Tell participants this is a game where you have to say you are bringing the correct items in order to come to the moon. I can bring a spoon but not a fork.

The trick: The things you can bring have to be words that contain double letters (i.e. spoon, door, reef, mirror). For example, "I can bring a glass but not a cup," or "I can bring a mitten but not a glove." To make it easier, you can accentuate the double letter sound, i.e. "I can bring a "spoooooooon."

4. Three Letter Body Parts:

Ask "Can you name 10 body parts that are spelled with three letters?" No slang allowed.

Answers: eye, hip, arm, leg, ear, toe, jaw, rib, gum, lip

5. Group Count:

Have the participants stand up and form a circle. Tell them to close their eyes. Ask them to try and count to 10 aloud as a group, but only one number can be said at a time in consecutive order. Whenever two people shout out any two numbers together, the group starts over. After a few attempts allow the group to open their eyes and try again.

6. 5 Popsicle Sticks:

Give participants a Ziploc bag of 10 Popsicle sticks.

Ask them:

- Can you make 5 Popsicle sticks into 2 triangles?
- Can you make 9 Popsicle sticks into 5 triangles?

You can find a ready made activity like this with even more craft stick puzzles on Teachers Pay Teachers by Playdough to Plato at www.teacherspayteachers.com/Product/STEM-Challenge-Craft-Stick-Puzzles-2828558.

7. Folded Paper Activity:

See this website for details, including a YouTube on how to set up the activity: https://blog.classcreator.io/teaching-kids-to-struggle-growthmindset.

This activity encourages a forced challenge by looking at a cut index card or half sheet of card stock. Ask students to remember what they saw while trying to figure out this challenge (Teacher/counselor can record what students are saying while trying to figure it out and then read it back for better processing).

Questions for discussion after activity:

- What would your boss/coach/teacher/parent think if they heard you saying these statements?
- If you were interviewing for a job or trying out for a competitive sports team, would these statements be helpful if your boss or coach heard you saying them?

8. Paper Clip Links:

This is a great trick that once you master, you can teach your students. Learn how to do it at: http://www.wikihow.com/Connect-Two-Paper-Clips-without-Touching-Them

Pipe Cleaner Perseverance Challenge

Materials: 10 pipe cleaners for each group, one gallon Ziploc bag, ruler, and a book on Grit (see page 113 for a selection of ideas).

Procedures:

1. Divide groups into teams of three to five people.
2. Distribute a gallon Ziploc filled with a bundle of 10 pipe-cleaners to each group.
3. Say, "This is a contest to see which team can build the "tallest structure" with the pipe cleaners in seven minutes. The structure cannot be held or wedged between desks/ tables. If a team breaks a rule, one pipe-cleaner will be taken away as a consequence.
4. After working for a few minutes say, "Freeze! Here's an additional challenge for you! Each team member must put one arm behind his/her back."
5. After a few more minutes, tell the teams they can now use both arms, but must continue the task without any talking (this helps with chaos level, as well).
6. Remind teams when there is one-minute left.
7. When time has run out, call, "Time's up!"
8. Measure each teams' creation with a yard stick or ruler to determine the tallest structure (add bonus points for cooperative teams if desired).
9. Talk about the qualities that often lead to success. Explain the definitions of grit and determination and ask for examples they noticed in themselves or teammates.
10. Read the book *GRIT and Bear It* or another book on the subject of grit, or watch "What Does Grit Mean" video http://bit.ly/2yDQd9i.

Extension Ideas:

Distribute "How Gritty are You?" worksheet (page 167). Review with students to see if answers match their behavior from this activity.

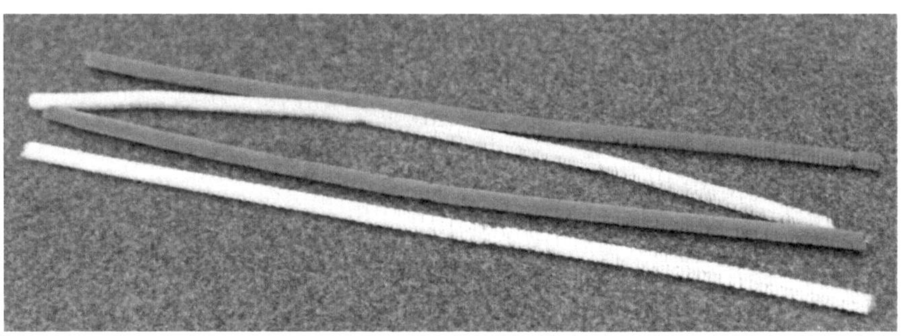

What evidence of

GROWTH MINDSET

do you see in playing this game?

Mindset Interviews

Think about someone you know who you can interview about the following topics. Ask them one of the questions in the "Things to ask" box. Write the answers in the "What did they say?" box below.

TOPIC	THINGS TO ASK	WHO DID YOU ASK?	WHAT DID THEY SAY?
Mindfulness			
Identify Brain Basics			
Not Yet is OK			
Determination and Grit			
Self-Talk			
Everyone is Unique			
Teach What You Know			

Integrating **Growth Mindset** *in Schools*

CHAPTER SIX

6

Using Data to Promote Your Program

Introduction to Chapter

Using Data

Data should be a key component in determining the efficacy of your programming. When working with students, it is important to make evidence-based decisions to drive your program. This chapter will review what types of data should be documented and provide a template for easy-to-replicate data collection.

Why Collect Data on Your Interventions?

1. **Prove Your Program Makes a Difference.** Prove the efficacy of what you are doing in a substantiated way.

2. **Provide Data that Makes Sense to Stakeholders.** School districts are often rich in data that is hard to understand. You can make data user-friendly and relevant to your school/ community.

3. **Give Your Administrators a Reason to Brag.** Let the leaders of your school be proud of what you are doing. If they have the documentation to show the innovation of your program, with graphs showing increased achievement, they will share it with others.

4. **Your Success Can Lead to More Innovation.** As you show how you are making a difference, your school leaders will give you more autonomy in creating innovative programs. Your efforts might also inspire innovation in other educators.

When Becky Grindstaff, a counselor at Tritt Elementary in Marietta, GA, shared her data with district administrators, the middle and high schools in their area reached out wanting to know how to implement growth mindset initiatives at their school. Positive achievement results interested decision makers at those schools. In the coming months, the schools are planning to get together to discuss the possibilities ahead. And it started with data collection that helped legitimize the growth mindset initiatives that are now being planned across grade levels.

"Because data can be used to "identify student needs, guide changes in instruction, motivate students, coach educators, evaluate programs and decisions, and communicate with parents and the public, educators can help ensure that the other measures they take to improve student learning are more effective."

How School District Leaders Can Support the Use of Data to Improve Teaching and Learning (April 2015); Chrys Dougherty, PhD April 2015 www.act.org

Three Types of Data

When collecting data, you should have a plan. Before you begin, let's review the different types of data. Page 161 gives a visual breakdown.

The three types of data are:

PROCESS, **PERCEPTION**, and **OUTCOME**

Process Data: These numbers tell the story of how many, who, and what. This data answers the question, "What did you do, and for whom?", and gives your program integrity and clarity. You'll be better equipped to answer questions like:

- How many students did you work with?
- How many lessons did you do with the students?
- How long were the lessons?
- How did you determine which students to work with?
- What curriculum did you use?

Perception Data: This is the data collected that tells what knowledge, attitudes, and skills were gained from an intervention. This data answers the question, "What do people think they know, believe, or can do?" These answers commonly come from questions or pre/post surveys given to participants (or their teachers/guardians).

Outcome Data: This is the results data of the intervention in terms of achievement, behavior, or attendance, and answers the question "Why does this matter?" This data often comes from discipline records, standardized testing, GPA, and/or attendance records. This is the information that administrators and parents will most want to receive and understand.

The above information is adapted from the Comprehensive National Model as per ASCA at https://www.schoolcounselor.org

Process Data

Who, What, How Many?

As measured by questions like:

- How many students?
- How many groups/lessons?
- What type of intervention?
- What was duration of group/ lessons?
- How were students selected?
- What grade level?

Example:
This small group included nine 4th grade students. The group met for 30 minute sessions over an eight week period of time.

Perception Data

Knowledge, Attitudes, and Skills

As measured by things like:

- Pre-Post Surveys
- Pre-Post Questionnaires filled out by Parents/Teachers
- Pre-Post Quizzes assessing knowledge gained

Example:
The pre-post survey given to students indicated that they had a better understanding of how the brain worked by 45%.

Outcome Data

Achievement, Behavior, Attendance

As measured by things like:

- Attendance Records
- Discipline Records
- Standardized Testing Scores
- Report Card Grades
- GPA
- SAT Scores
- Graduation Rates

Example:
Discipline referrals decreased by 52% over the span of this group with these students. Also, 75% of the students had an increase in positive conduct grades on report cards.

How to Collect Data for your Classroom, Group, or Program

It is important to understand some math basics here. Luckily, there are websites to help.

When you are looking at your perception data (pre/post surveys) or outcome data (test scores/discipline referrals, etc.), you can use the template on page 163. You can also create an excel file to easily make graphs.

One important thing with data is remembering to accurately calculate the percentage change. Trish Hatch, the guru of school counseling data collection, teaches this statistical formula as the "David Effect." This formula will help you understand that if a pre-test is scored 50 and a post-test is scored 100, that would be a 100% increase.

1. *Pre-test number correct or beginning # = A*
2. *Post test number correct or final # = B*
3. *B - A = C (change)*
4. *C / A = D (decimal change)*
5. *Move decimal two digits to right to get the % of change*

Hatch, T. & Holland, L. (2003) Moreno Valley School Counselor Academy, Moreno Valley, Ca.

BUT WAIT... THE INTERNET CAN HELP!!

Just plug pre and post test scores into a website like the one below. It will give you a percentage of change.

http://www.percentagecalculator.net/

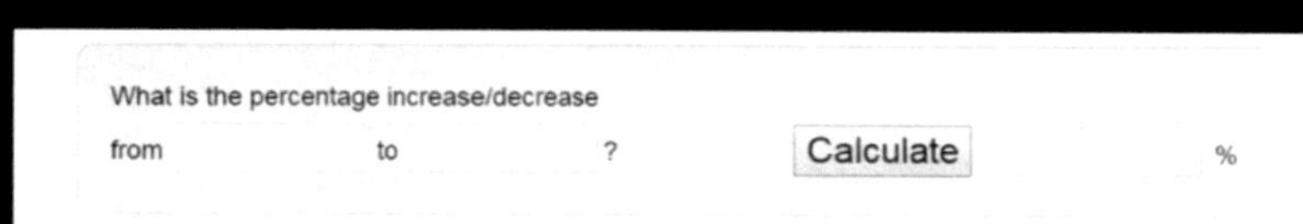

Data Collection

Each school is different, but we all use assessments. Choose the measure that is right for you to track student growth.

STUDENT NAME	PRE	POST	PERCENTAGE CHANGE
Student 1			
Student 2			
Student 3			
Student 4			
Student 5			
Student 6			
AVERAGE			

Examples of Surveys that Can Be Used For Pre/Post/Perception Data

Which Surveys are Here?

Mindset Survey for Parent/Teacher (page 165)

For the parents/guardians of students involved in:

- Mindset Mentors
- Mindset Advisement
- Small Group

Mindset Self-Assessment (page 166)

How Gritty Are You? (page 167)

What do You Know about Growth Mindset? Pre/Post Test (page 168)

Can be used for:

- Mindset Mentors
- Mindset Advisement
- Classroom Lessons
- Small Group

Mindset Survey for Parent/Teacher

Can be Used for Pre/Post Assessment

Name____Date _____________________

Name of Adult Completing this Form______________________________________

On a scale of 1-5, how you would rate this student on the following statements:

	STRONGLY AGREE	AGREE	NOT SURE	DISAGREE	STRONGLY DISAGREE
1. He/she is determined and has an "I won't give up" work ethic.	5	4	3	2	1
2. He/she handles it appropriately if they make mistakes.	5	4	3	2	1
3. He/she can calm down if angry.	5	4	3	2	1
4. He/she has a good attitude about school.	5	4	3	2	1
5. He/she seems to have friends.	5	4	3	2	1
6. He/she has positive self-esteem.	5	4	3	2	1
7. He/she has good study skills.	5	4	3	2	1
8. He/she has the mindset that they can accomplish any task when focused.	5	4	3	2	1

Mindset Self-Assessment

Can be Used for Pre/Post Assessment

Name____Date ____________________

On a scale of 1-5, how you would rate this student on the following statements:

	STRONGLY AGREE	AGREE	NOT SURE	DISAGREE	STRONGLY DISAGREE
1. I am determined and have an "I won't give up" work ethic.	5	4	3	2	1
2. I handle it appropriately if I make mistakes.	5	4	3	2	1
3. I can calm down if angry.	5	4	3	2	1
4. I have a good attitude about school.	5	4	3	2	1
5. I have friends.	5	4	3	2	1
6. I have positive self-esteem.	5	4	3	2	1
7. I have good study skills.	5	4	3	2	1
8. I can accomplish any task I set my mind to.	5	4	3	2	1

Name ______________________________ Date______________

How Gritty are You?

Directions: Circle the answer that best describes you on a scale of 1-5, according to the descriptions above the numbers. Remember there are no right or wrong answers.

	Strongly Agree	Agree	Not Sure/ Sometimes	Disagree	Strongly Disagree
1. I have been able to work through some hard things.	5	4	3	2	1
2. I am embarrassed to ask my teacher for help when I need it.	5	4	3	2	1
3. I am very focused on getting my work done.	5	4	3	2	1
4. When things don't go my way, I keep on working and don't let it get me down.	5	4	3	2	1
5. I can stay focused, even when something is boring.	5	4	3	2	1
6. I am a hard-working person.	5	4	3	2	1
7. I have many activities that I'm really interested in.	5	4	3	2	1
8. Long assignments are difficult for me.	5	4	3	2	1
9. I always finish what I start.	5	4	3	2	1
10. Even when classwork is difficult, I work at it until I get it done.	5	4	3	2	1

Now, write the number that you circled for the following questions:

Question 1 ________

Question 3 ________

Question 4 ________

Question 6 ________

Question 9 ________

Question 10 ________

Total when I add the underlined numbers = ________

Adapted from the 12 point GRIT scale: Duckworth, A.L., Peterson, C., Matthews, M.D., & Kelly, D.R. (2007). Grit: Perseverance and passion for long-term goals. Journal of Personality and Social Psychology, 9, 1087-1101.

See below for a scale of how GRITTY you are:

30-28
You are the grittiest of the gritty.

27-25
You definitely have grit, lots of it.

24-20
You try and keep trying.

19-13
Most of the time, you give your best effort.

12-6
You need to focus a bit more on trying your best.

What Do You Know about Growth Mindset?
Pre/Post Test

Name____Date _____________________

1. When we discuss how grit helps us succeed, what does it mean to "have grit?"
    a. To have a problem that is getting in the way of success.
    b. To eat a warm breakfast to help us stay healthy.
    c. To have perseverance to stick with a task over time, even when it is difficult.
2. How can the "Power of Yet" help you in life?
    a. It reminds you to not give up
    b. It reminds you to rest and relax
    c. It reminds you to complete your work on time
3. Neuroplasticity is a term that means:
    a. Brain cells, called neurons, respond better when you hold items that are plastic.
    b. Your brain can grow with hard work and practice.
    c. We are all born with a certain amount of "smarts" and neurons and brains do not change over time.
4. I could teach other people about how the brain works.
    a. No, not at all
    b. I know a little bit
    c. Yes
5. People would say I have a good attitude.
    a. All the time
    b. Some of the time
    c. Never
6. It is okay if I make mistakes.
    a. No
    b. Sometimes
    c. Yes
7. I am smart.
    a. No, I'm not smart
    b. I am smart at some things
    c. Yes, I am smart
8. I can be anything I want to be if I work hard enough.
    a. Yes
    b. No
    c. I don't know

Why Create a Results Report?

In my district, where I have worked for 20 years, we are lucky to have been trained on how to deliver a comprehensive school counseling program (thanks to our advocates and supervisors, Gail Smith and Julie Hartline). After having that training, it is easy to see the value in collecting data. Many districts don't require data reports, but I am glad my district requires at least one report per year, because we have learned a great deal from having to do it, and also receiving the formative and constructive feedback on these reports. It has created a growth mindset experience for my PLC of the Cobb County School Counselors. We learn and grow from being pushed. As an added bonus, administrators often see those who share and post data as professional and innovative in going above and beyond.

The American School Counselors Association RAMP (Recognized ASCA Model Program) Schools have mandatory results reports to hand in. Data is part of the National Model from ASCA.

Check out more at www.schoolcounselor.org

Sharing Data as a Growth Mindset PLC

Question: What is a PLC?

> **Answer:** PLC stands for Professional Learning Community (sometimes called Professional Learning Networks or Collaborative Learning Communities). According to www.edglossary.org, "A professional learning community, or PLC, is a group of educators that meets regularly, shares expertise, and works collaboratively to improve teaching skills and the academic performance of students. The term is also applied to schools or teaching faculties that use small-group collaboration as a form of professional development."

Professional Learning Communities are an educational best practice in collaborating to better your own craft. What could be more "growth mindset" than learning from others? If you are in a district that has PLC's, or if you are part of a PLC on social media, think about creating a Growth Mindset PLC.

A Growth Mindset PLC is a great way to get together with colleagues to discuss implementing growth mindset lessons for group or core curriculum and begin collecting data simultaneously. This not only shows a larger sample size, but also highlights the efforts of your PLC.

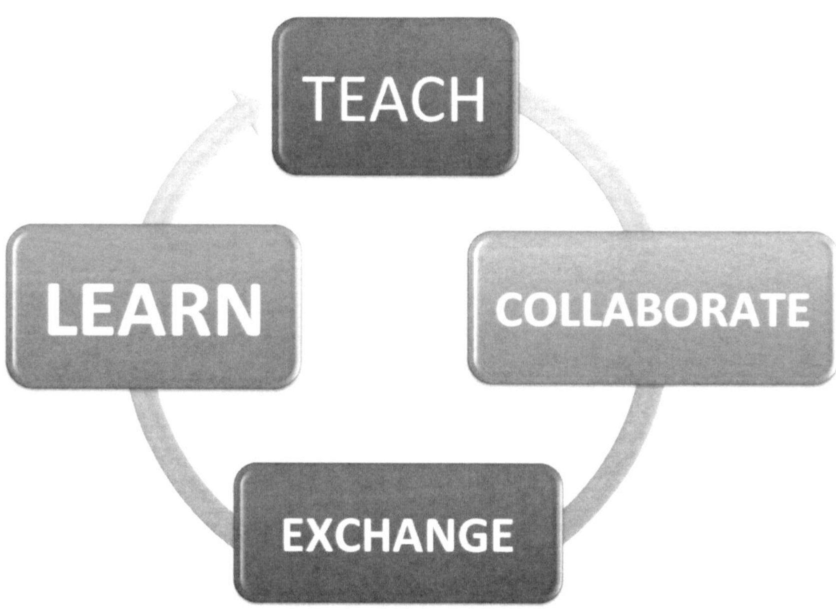

TEMPLATE

Data Results Report

Use an extra sheet if needed.

Date: ____________________ School: ______________________________________

Name of Educators Implementing Program:

____

Topic: ____

Purpose of Intervention: ____

____

Intended Student Outcome: ____

____

____

PROCESS DATA

How Many Students? ______________ Grade Level? ______________________

Materials/Curriculum Used: ____

____

Procedures/Description of Lessons: ______________________________________

____

____

Perception Data: ____

____

Outcome Data (*Attach a graph if possible*): _____________________________

____

SUMMARY

What have you concluded from the delivery of the curriculum? ______________

____

Based on your conclusions, what is your next step? _________________________

____

SAMPLE

Data Results Report

Use an extra sheet if needed.

Date: 2015-16 School: Blackwell ES

Name of Educators Implementing Program:
Lisa King

Topic: Mindset Matters: Growth Mindset Curriculum

Purpose of Intervention: To have students acquire an understanding that they can train their brain to grow (the concept of neuroplasticity) which can lead to positive academic results.

Intended Student Outcome: The intended outcome is that students increase their understanding of how practicing skills can help the brain grow (intended growth is 10% increase in perception). It is also intended that the increased student perception will lead to increase in Level 3 and 4 End of Grade (EOG) Standardized Test in ELA scores by 10%.

PROCESS DATA

How Many Students? 126 Grade Level? 4th grade

Materials/Curriculum Used: "Mindset Matters" (King, 2016)

Procedures/Description of Lessons: Four lessons from the curriculum "Mindset Matters" (King, 2016) were used to teach growth mindset in 4th grade. These lessons were: Lesson 1: Mindfulness; Lesson 2: Identify Brain Basics; Lesson 3: Not Yet is OK; Lesson 4: Determination and Grit

Perception Data: A pre/post assessment of the student's knowledge and attitudes. A true/false survey (Pre: September 2015/Post: March 2016) determined students change in knowledge and attitude.

Outcome Data (*Attach a graph if possible*): Outcome Data was determined by the ELA scores of the Milestones EOG to see if Level 3 and Level 4 scores increased from the prior year.

See Outcome Data Graphs on next page.

SUMMARY

What have you concluded from the delivery of the curriculum? See next page.

Based on your conclusions, what is your next step? See next page.

Outcome Data attached to report.

The data below reflects the % of students that answered "True" on a True/False pre/post survey:

Pre %	Post %	% Change	Question
51	50	-2%	1. I know a lot about how the brain works.
14	86	514%	2. I am <u>interested</u> in how the brain works.
43	98	128%	3. I think my brain can grow, the more I practice different skills.
41	79	93%	4. When kids know about how their brain works, they actually do better in school.

As the students learned about their brain and that skill practice can increase their neuroplasticity and ability, we can look to see if their achievement scores were impacted by these lessons. When looking at Milestone Data to see the increase in % of students meeting/exceeding standards on the end-of-year standardized test, we see that our Level 4 and Level 3 learners increased significantly from these students 3rd grade scores in 2015 to their 4th grade scores in 2016.

MILESTONE SCORES FOR ELA

	2015	2016	
LEVEL 4	12%	20%	+66.7%
LEVEL 3	30%	40%	+33.3%

MILESTONE SCORES FOR MATH

	2015	2016	
LEVEL 4	5%	21%	+320%
LEVEL 3	33%	41	+24.2%

Continued from Data Results Report...

What have you concluded from the delivery of the curriculum?

The students in 4th grade had an extraordinary increase in both knowledge and attitudes, as per the pre/post survey for questions 2,3, and 4 of the student survey (see below). On question #1 that asks "Do you know how your brain works?" there was a decrease. Potentially the student's new understanding of the complexities of the brain and the realization that there is so much more to know could have caused this. Looking at the positive outcomes, I believe that students love to learn about metacognition and that with the support of the 4th grade teachers continuing to talk about the concepts of Growth Mindset and Grit in their classrooms, the students yielded positive outcomes in perception data and achievement data.

Based on your conclusions, what is your next step?

The success of the *Mindset Matters* Curriculum has been exciting and positive. Next year, as I loop with these 4th graders to 5th grade, we will continue to use this curriculum to expand the student's sense of self-efficacy in being able to "grow their brain" by practicing skills they want to improve. Additionally, I would like to look more closely at outcome results of Milestones Reading and Math Scores to determine if the % of students who can move from Level 3 and 4 can be maintained and even increased. Plans will also include a professional development workshop for teachers, so they can include growth mindset concepts in their classrooms.

Advocating for Your Program

Sharing results data is a great way to advocate for your program. Whether you are a teacher or school counselor, it is important for you to show how you are working to implement programs that benefit students. What better way to show how students are benefiting than showing the numbers? And even if every student doesn't improve (which they won't always), your data collection is forcing you to examine what best practices are or are not working.

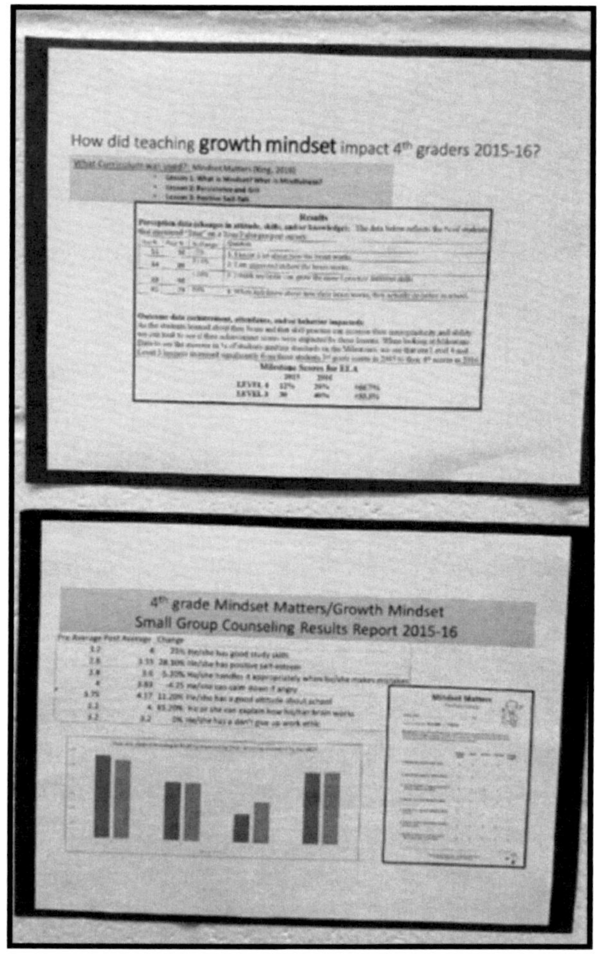

Ways you can share your results:

- Email your results to stakeholders
- Post results near your office

"According to Aimee Rogstad Guidera, CEO of Data Quality Campaign, collecting student data is an important factor in increasing student achievement. Guidera says, student data helps keep both parents and the community in the loop about how schools are serving its students."

Source: Gorman, N. E 2015, 'Why Collecting Student Data Is Important to Student Achievement', Education World.)

WOOP and Final Thoughts

You've done it! You're taking the first, intentional steps towards integrating growth mindset into your learning community. I know it can be overwhelming to think about the steps and time involved, but take it one step at a time, and you'll be there before you know it!

Create an Action Plan...WOOP!

As you think over what parts of the growth mindset initiative you want to implement at your school, write down an action plan.

Which of these programs do you hope to begin? When?

Now think about **WOOP**. What is **WOOP**? It is a strategy developed by Gabriel Oettingen, a professor at NYU, that helps people with goal setting. This framework, adopted by the Character Lab (with resources from them available at www.characterlab.org/woop/) helps people think through their **W**ish, **O**utcome, **O**bstacle, **P**lan--- their **WOOP**. Not only is **WOOP** another great strategy to introduce to our students, but it is also a great strategy for us to use with our action plan "wish" written above.

Wish ____

____

Outcome ____

____

Obstacle ____

____

Plan ____

____

Here's to you as you launch into bringing growth mindset to your school community! If you have questions along the way, feel free to reach out to me online. Use the resources I've posted for you at https://ncyi.org/shop/integratingmindset/. Get a partner who's excited to work alongside you in weaving this into your school's programs. Each day, you'll see progress, and you'll know that change is happening!

Best, Lisa

"Mindset change is not about picking up a few pointers here and there. It's about seeing things in a new way. When people...change to a growth mindset, they change from a judge-and-be-judged framework to a learn-and-help-learn framework. Their commitment is to growth, and growth takes plenty of time, effort, and mutual support."

Carol S. Dweck

Mindset: The New Psychology of Success

Integrating **Growth Mindset** *in Schools*

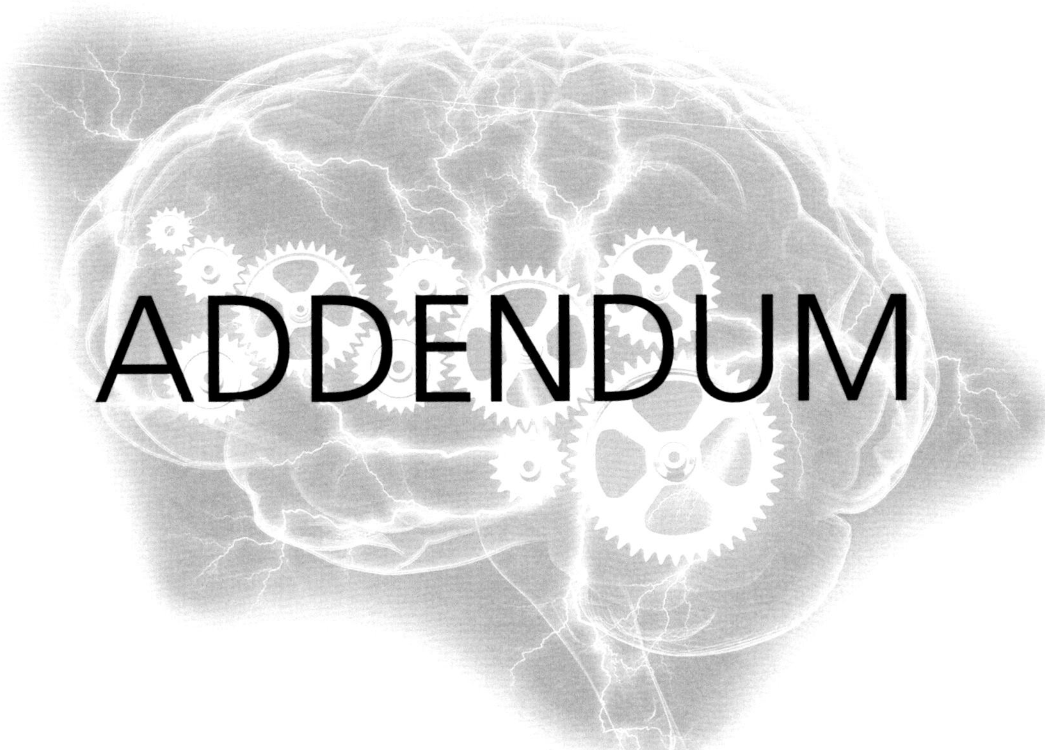

ADDENDUM

Mini Posters to Create a Common Language

Mindset Meter

- **YES, I DID IT!**
- **I will do it.**
- **I can do it!**
- **I'll try to do it.**
- **How do I do it?**
- **I can't do it.**
- **I won't do it!**

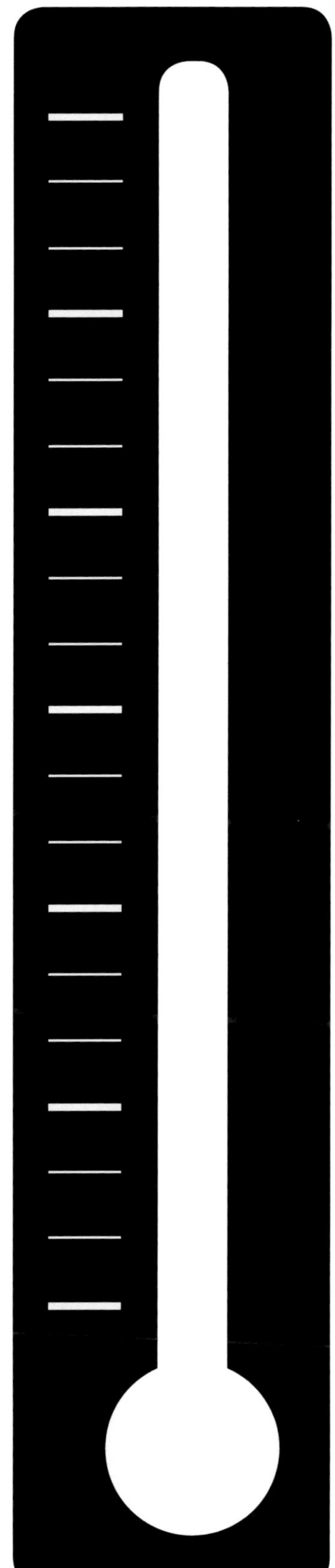

If you are starting to think

I CAN'T DO THIS...

Don't forget to add

YET.

What can I do to
mprove the next time?

How can I tackle this challenge?

What solutions have I thought about trying, but not tried yet?

What questions can I ask myeslf when I want to deal with a problem the Growth Mindset way?

Did I make a mistake that I can fix?

Is there a creative way I can solve the problem?

What can I learn from this problem?

WHAT IS A GOOD WAY TO HANDLE FRUSTRATION WHEN SOMETHING IS DIFFICULT?

FAIL just means:
First
Attempt
In
Learning

So, ***TRY AGAIN***!

Take Deep Mindful Breaths.

If possible, give yourself a break and come back to it later.

Say to yourself, "I just can't do this **YET**."